ROYAL HORTICULTURAL SOCIETY

Pests and diseases

Andrew Halstead
and Béatrice Henricot

LONDON, NEW YORK, MUNICH, MELBOURNE, DELHI

PROJECT EDITOR Emma Callery
PROJECT ART EDITOR Alison Shackleton
SENIOR EDITOR Helen Fewster
MANAGING EDITOR Esther Ripley
MANAGING ART EDITOR Alison Donovan
PICTURE RESEARCH Ria Jones, Frances Vargo
PRODUCTION EDITORS Kavita Varma, Tony Phipps

First published in Great Britain in 2010 by
Dorling Kindersley Ltd
Penguin Books Ltd
80 Strand
London WC2R 0RL

2 4 6 8 10 9 7 5 3 1

ISBN 978-1-4053-4886-7

Printed and bound by Star Standard Industries Pte Ltd,
Singapore

To find out more about RHS membership, contact:
RHS Membership Department
PO Box 313, London SW1P 2PE

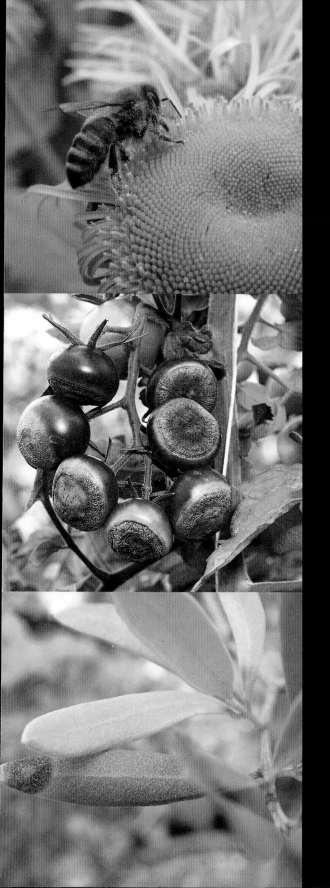

Contents

Healthy gardening   6
Give your plants tender, loving care and they
find it easier to fight off pests and diseases

What are pests and diseases?   24
Know which pests and diseases are likely to
occur and they will be easier to control

Controlling pests and diseases   50
Fight off attacks with chemical and non-
chemical treatments

Trees, shrubs, and climbers   64
Swiftly identify problems by checking out
these larger plants, divided into three groups

The herbaceous garden   88
Smaller plants are just as susceptible to pests
and diseases as trees, shrubs, and climbers

The productive garden   106
Keep your vegetable and fruit losses to a
minimum by being vigilant

Glasshouses   132
In warm environments, infection can take
hold quickly: learn how to prevent this

Index   140
Acknowledgements   144

Andrew Halstead and
Béatrice Henricot
Andrew Halstead is the RHS's Principal
Entomologist and Béatrice Henricot is Principal
Pathologist. They both have many years of
experience of identifying and dealing with
garden pests and diseases.

Healthy gardening

The healthy growth of plants can be affected by pests and diseases, nutrient deficiencies, and disorders caused by environmental stresses. It is generally the case that if you grow your plants well, they are less likely to succumb to pests and diseases. Selecting resistant varieties, AGM plants, or generally vigorous plants will help to prevent problems. Also choose suitable plants for the soil and position of your garden, and give them plenty of water, otherwise they may be permanently damaged or even killed. Good garden husbandry helps to prevent pests and diseases from taking hold.

The benefits of healthy gardening

Growing a wide range of plants can reduce the impact of pests and diseases. Some plants may suffer damage, but others spared. Where large numbers of a few plants are grown, it is easier for pests and diseases to cause serious damage.

Pictures clockwise from far left

Fruit trees Long-lived plants, such as fruit trees and bushes, can build up pest and disease problems over the years. Look out for aphids, mildews, and virus diseases. Put up a tit nest box as these birds will collect hundreds of caterpillars a day while they are rearing their chicks.

Flower borders Flower beds planted with annuals, bulbs, and herbaceous plants provide interest through most of the year. Plants in flower from spring to autumn support butterflies and bees, providing them with nectar and pollen. Bees are essential pollinating insects for many fruits and other plants.

Vegetable gardens Growing some ornamental plants, such as African or French marigolds, close to vegetables will attract hoverflies and other aphid predators, which will help to control aphids on beans and other susceptible plants. Crop rotation helps to avoid the build up of some vegetable pests and diseases, especially those that are soil-borne.

Garden ponds Pond plants have few significant pests or diseases. The presence of water adds a valuable habitat for frogs, toads, and newts, which helps in the control of slugs and insect pests.

Long grass Most grass in gardens is maintained as mown lawn, but some can be allowed as an informal meadow area. Native meadow wild flowers can be grown to encourage insects, birds, and other wildlife by providing shelter, and food in the form of nectar, pollen, and seeds.

Right plant, right place

Plants differ in the conditions required for optimum growth. Before planting a garden, consider factors such as the soil type, drainage, whether it has a sunny or shaded aspect, and how cold the winters will be. Plants that prefer, or at least tolerate, the local conditions are more likely to thrive and will be more resistant to pests and diseases.

Pictures clockwise from right

Sunny gardens Sunny conditions suit the majority of garden plants, giving gardeners a wide choice of fruits, vegetables, and ornamental plants to grow. Sunny gardens can also be dry gardens, especially in sandy and other free-draining soils. In such situations, it is wise to select drought-tolerant plants to avoid the need for frequent watering. A mulch of rotted compost or other organic material on the soil surface helps retain soil moisture throughout the year.

Shaded gardens Shade can be provided by buildings, tall fences, walls, hedges, or trees. With trees and hedges, there is the added problem of these larger plants taking most of the available moisture and nutrients from the soil. Plants that need good light are likely to grow in a spindly fashion in heavy shade. The plants best suited for these conditions are spring bulbs, ferns, and ornamental plants that naturally grow in woodland situations.

Acidic and alkaline soils Some plants, such as heathers, rhododendrons, azaleas, and camellias, need an acidic soil with a pH value of less than 7 (*see p.14*). If grown in an alkaline or chalky soil, where the pH value will be 7 or more, the foliage becomes yellow and the plants are likely to die. While most plants can be grown in acidic soils, the choice for alkaline soils is more restricted.

Coastal gardens Gardens near the coast are frequently windswept and plants can be damaged by salt spray. It is often necessary to plant a shelter belt of wind-tolerant trees or shrubs in order to provide more favourable conditions for the rest of the garden. Coastal gardens can enjoy a much milder climate than those inland, which means that half hardy or tender plants can successfully be grown out of doors.

Choosing your plants

When it comes to susceptibility to pests and diseases, not all plants are equal. Well grown and vigorous plants are less likely to suffer problems. Some cultivars have been bred to be resistant or more tolerant of certain pests and diseases.

Pictures clockwise from left

Resistant plants Roses suffer from several debilitating fungal diseases, such as mildew, black spot, and rust. These diseases require regular treatment with fungicides throughout the growing season. Fortunately, some roses have been bred that are resistant to or relatively little affected by these diseases. Other resistant fruits, vegetables, and ornamental plants are available and it is worth looking for such cultivars in seed and nursery catalogues.

Specialist nurseries Plants obtained from a specialist nursery may be more expensive than from a supermarket garden section, but are often of better quality. The grower is also likely to be able to supply expert knowledge on the best ways to grow and care for the plants.

AGM plants The Royal Horticultural Society gives the Award of Garden Merit (AGM) to cultivars of fruits, vegetables, and ornamental plants that are considered to be excellent cultivars for garden cultivation. The selection is made by a panel of experts, and factors taken into consideration include the plant having a good constitution and being particularly resistant to pests or diseases. Plants or cultivars with AGM status have a trophy symbol on the plant label or in catalogues: ♔. By choosing AGM plants, you will have higher quality plants in your garden and avoid some of the inferior cultivars that are available.

Choose healthy plants Look carefully at plants before you buy them. Select those with a healthy appearance and a good growth habit. Avoid plants with yellowing or wilted foliage, or those that have grown too tall for their pots. A dense growth of moss or weeds on the soil surface tells you that the plant has been on the sale bench a long time. Pick bulbs and corms that are large, firm, and without signs of decay or dryness. Look for signs of pests or diseases and don't take them home with you!

Understanding the nutrients in your soil

A good soil provides water, air, and nutrients for healthy plant growth. Not all soils are ideal for every kind of cultivation, but they can be improved. Choose plants that are suited to your soil characteristics, but first establish the type of soil in your garden.

What is soil? Soil is formed from the breakdown of rocks into particles of sand, silt, and clay. These particles make up half the soil volume, the rest is filled with air, water, living organisms, and humus. Types of garden soils can be defined by the proportion of sand, silt, and clay particles they contain and their pH. The ideal soil for gardeners is loam, which contains sand, silt, and clay in relatively even concentrations. Soil is the source of plant mineral nutrients. Those required in high quantities are nitrogen, phosphorus, and potassium (NPK). Other important nutrients, such as calcium, sulphur, iron, and boron, are required in small quantities. The nutrient content of any soil can be improved using fertilizers (*see p.19*).

pH test

A pH test is a means of chemically testing the acidity or alkalinity of a soil. Very generally, an acid soil has a pH value below 7.7 is considered neutral, and above 7, the soil is alkaline. Soil pH influences the availability of nutrients to plants. Many ornamental plants grow best in soil at about pH 7; for most vegetables, a pH 6–6.5 is suitable (brassicas prefer a pH 7.5). Lime-hating plants, such as heather, rhododendrons, and camellias, prefer a pH 5.1–6.

Chemical soil kits available in most garden centres are easy to use to check the pH values of the soil in the garden.

Sandy soil A sandy soil has large particles surrounded by air spaces. It tends to be gritty and fall apart in your hand when rolled into a ball. It is easy to cultivate and warms up quickly in the spring, but it dries out fast and minerals and nutrients are leached easily. Acidification can occur rapidly as the calcium is washed out easily. Adding organic matter (*see p.16*) improves water retention, fertility, and structure. Mulching reduces evaporation and erosion.

Clay soil A clay soil tends to be sticky when wet. Take a handful of moist topsoil, squeeze it into a ball and if it keeps its shape, it has a high clay content. It is reluctant to dry, but when it does, it can set hard, shrink, and crack. In general, clay soil has good nutrient concentrations but it can become waterlogged, resulting in root problems. Clay soil benefits from organic matter. Non-organic material, such as horticultural grit and perlite, helps its structure.

The effects of nutrient deficiency

Nitrogen deficiency causes leaves to be small and chlorotic, they may turn yellow or red, and growth is reduced. It is more common in heavily cropped soil or one with low organic content. Unrotted organic matter, such as wood chippings, may deprive the soil of nitrogen.

Phosphorus deficiency causes reduction in flowering and fruiting, and, in general, poor plant growth. The leaves develop a purplish discolouration, are small, and fall early. Phosphorus deficiency is most commonly seen on acid soils or following heavy rain or watering.

Potassium deficiency causes leaf scorching and curling. Flowers and fruit may be reduced. Plants that require a lot of potassium, such as tomatoes (deficiency causes blotchy ripening), beans, and fruits, are more likely to suffer. It is more common on sandy, peaty, or chalky soils.

Calcium deficiency is often seen in acid soils or any inadequately watered soil, which prevents the plant taking up calcium. Commonly, it causes blossom end rot of tomatoes, shown as a black patch at the fruit's flower end, and bitter pit of apples, where dark spots appear under the skin.

Iron deficiency causes yellowing between the leaf veins and is more apparent on young leaves. In severe cases, leaves look white and scorching of the margins and tips occur. Often seen with manganese deficiency, it commonly occurs when acid-loving plants are grown in alkaline soils.

Magnesium deficiency causes the older leaves to yellow between the veins, sometimes with brown areas (necrosis). In severe cases, leaves may wither and fall, leading to a loss of crop. It is typically seen on sandy soils during wet periods. Magnesium is made unavailable by excess potassium.

Looking after your soil

There is a variety of soil improvers to amend difficult soils. Fertilizers provide a concentrated supply of one or more plant nutrients, but they have little impact on the soil structure. Soil conditioners, like farmyard manure and garden compost, have low fertilizer value, but they condition the soil.

Digging in organic matter

Animal manures are useful for heavy and light soils alike. They need to be composted for at least a year as they release ammonia, which can scorch young or tender plants. Dig them into the soil in the autumn.

Plant waste, such as garden compost and composted bark, improves soil texture and contributes to fertility. Apply as with manures. Spent mushroom compost is a good soil conditioner but not around lime-hating plants due to its chalk content. Leafmould is excellent for structurally improving soils, but low in nutritional value.

Plants grown as manure crops (green manures) are good options for fallow areas. They provide ground cover to smother weeds and to store soil nutrients, preventing leaching during non-crop periods. When the land is needed, dig the green manure plant back in so it rots down, releasing nutrients and adding organic matter.

Mulching

Mulches are a loose covering of biodegradable or non-biodegradable materials. They suppress weeds, improve moisture retention, and regulate soil temperature.

Biodegradable mulches, such as compost, manure, leafmould, and bark, play the most important role in soil management. They add organic matter to the soil as opposed to non-biodegradable mulches, such as plastic sheeting, gravel, or glass chippings.

All organic mulches decompose completely in the soil due to the activities of soil-borne organisms, such as worms and saprophytic fungi. As a result, the structure of the soil and the nutrient availability is improved.

Before applying a mulch it is essential that the soil is wet and warm. The mulch should be spread evenly. Soil structure can be improved with a layer as thin as 1cm (½in), but to control weeds effectively an 8–10cm (3–4in) layer of mulch is needed. Keep any mulch clear of the stems of woody plants.

Composting

Composting is a biochemical process whereby organic matter is decomposed by naturally occurring organisms to produce a stable, soil-like end product called compost. It provides a means of converting waste materials from both the kitchen and garden into a free, environmentally friendly source of organic matter, which can be used to improve soil fertility, conserve soil moisture, and enhance plant growth. It also helps the community as a whole by reducing landfill.

The microorganisms involved in the composting process need air, moisture, and nitrogen to efficiently decompose the organic matter. This is why air should be allowed in from the sides and base of the compost heap. If the heap shows signs of drying out, apply water. Moisture can be encouraged to stay in the heap by lining it with sacking, old carpet, or polythene.

A compost heap is ideally placed in a sheltered and shady area. There are many types of homemade and proprietary compost bins. For good results, they should be around 1.2m (4ft) tall and can be much wider than they are high. Once the material is of dark crumbly texture it is ready to use, a process that can take up to two years depending on the temperature of the heap.

Add kitchen waste Kitchen and garden waste makes good compost if properly mixed, but do not let one particular component build up. Ideally make the compost a mix of one third of soft, green and sappy material (grass clippings, raw vegetables peelings, tea leaves) and two thirds of hard brown materials (twigs, straw, newspapers).

Composting worms Unlike most earthworms, these are striped and live in decaying organic matter. At least 100 worms are needed to start a worm compost bin. They are more productive at 18–25°C (64–77°F) in compost that is moist but not too wet. The bins should have a large surface area, be rainproof, insulated, and well ventilated.

Good garden hygiene

Healthy plants are more able to fight off pests and diseases. Recently planted or propagated plants are most vulnerable, so take extra care to protect them.

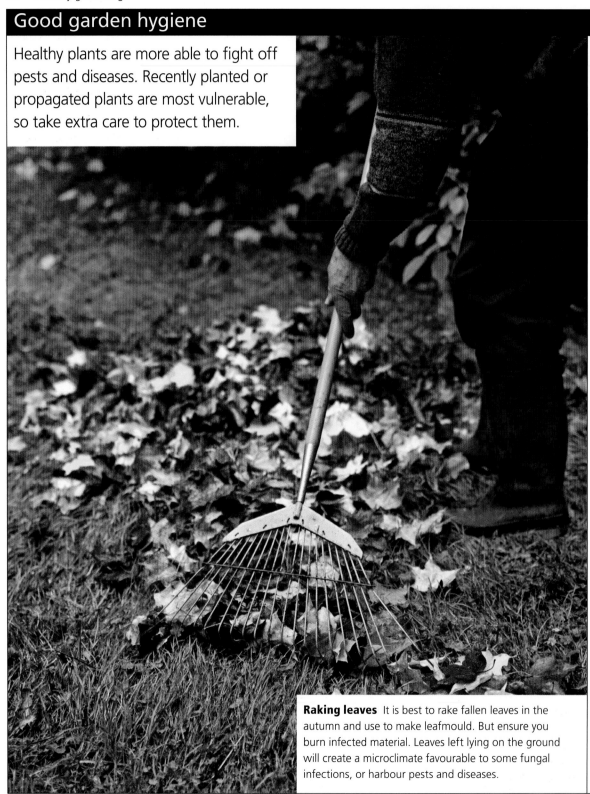

Raking leaves It is best to rake fallen leaves in the autumn and use to make leafmould. But ensure you burn infected material. Leaves left lying on the ground will create a microclimate favourable to some fungal infections, or harbour pests and diseases.

Caring for your plants

Good hygiene is important to avoid a build-up of pests and diseases in the garden. Soaking pots in a garden disinfectant followed by a rinse of water helps avoid fungal infections. To ensure healthy growth, sow seeds at the appropriate time and always give new plants plenty of water, which is the most common cause of failure of newly established plants. Wiping tools after pruning plants is a good practice, too. If the plants are diseased, clean tools even more frequently. Many diseases and pests overwinter on fallen material so their removal after the growing season gives your plants a better chance to grow healthily in the spring.

Sterilizing Using cutting tools on an infected plant and then on a healthy one without disinfecting them can spread disease. Similarly pots, trays, and work surfaces should be cleaned with disinfectant to minimize the spread of pests and diseases.

Feeding This is usually done when plants grow rapidly during the spring and early summer. Organic fertilizers provide a variety of nutrients whereas inorganic or man-made fertilizers can be general purpose, containing equal quantities of NPK, or single nutrient compounds.

Watering This is important during the critical stages of a plant's development, such as seedlings and when flowers and fruits are being produced. Water in the evening to minimize soil evaporation and apply it at the base of plants, not on the foliage, to reduce risk of foliar diseases.

Weeding Weeds will outcompete the plants we want to grow as ornamentals and crops by depriving them of nutrients, water, and light. They are also reservoirs for some pests and diseases (such as viruses). Aim to remove weeds before they set seeds.

Pruning for health

Poor pruning can increase the likelihood of infection from disease and, to some extent, pests. Equally, some types of pruning are carried out only with a view to removing diseased or infested plant material.

Why prune?

Pruning is carried out to conform a plant to a specified size and shape, to remove excess branches to prevent them rubbing together, and to remove broken, damaged, or diseased branches or double leaders. Pruning also gives the opportunity to remove very thin or crossing shoots from the centre. This will open up the centre of the plant and allow more light and air to flow through the crown.

Most homeowners should limit tree pruning to small branches that can be reached from the ground. For large branches, ensure that you involve professional tree experts with proper equipment.

Remove dead/diseased wood If the branches are dying from a stem infection, such as nectria canker, silver leaf, and coral spot, the infection may be removed if the diseased wood is cut out promptly. This also reduces the possibility of new infections taking hold.

Crossing and rubbing branches Branches that cross or rub, damage the bark, creating entry points for pathogens such as wood decay fungi. Prune out these branches and apply a wound sealant if wounding occurs during the dormant season.

Thin dense growth Improving air ventilation in this way reduces the chance of infection of many air-borne fungi. Reduce the older stems of flowering shrubs by one third every year to stimulate the production of new shoots and create a microclimate less favourable to infection.

Correct cuts

Remove branches correctly by cutting them with clean, sharp tools, since rough cuts or torn branches can promote disease development. Also use good quality secateurs to prune stems up to pencil size thickness, but use then use loppers or pruning saws for anything larger. Loppers and pruning saws are designed to cut through wood smoothly and cleanly. Pole pruners with telescopic handles can be used for high branches from the ground, and chain saws can be used on the largest of branches. However, chain saws are best avoided by the homeowner. You must always wear gloves when pruning and burn diseased material.

Make sure that you cut branches at a slant next to a bud that can produce new growth and do not make cuts flush with the trunk.

In the past, part of the standard recommendation for pruning has been to apply a wound paint to all fresh cuts. This treatment is now less in favour as it is believed that it interferes with the healing process. However, the treatment might still be useful to protect wounds that occur in the dormant season.

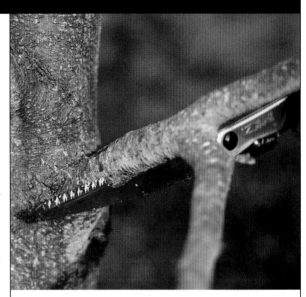

Remove branches correctly Do not cut off branches absolutely flush from the stem as this will impair the growth of the scar tissue. It is best to make the cut just outside the swollen area at the base of the branch that sometimes has a bark ridge.

Cut out unhealthy branches These cuts are usually best carried out as soon as the symptoms are seen rather than waiting for the appropriate pruning time. Make the cut well below the infected tissue, which can be recognized as being stained below the bark.

Prune above an outward facing bud Always prune above a strong bud or healthy side shoot to create an open, uncongested centre. The cut should slope away from the bud or shoot. Pruning too close to a bud will cause damage and too far away will result in die-back.

Vegetable gardens

Rotating groups of vegetables on a three- or four-year plan is a simple procedure that prevents the build up of pests and diseases without the use of chemicals.

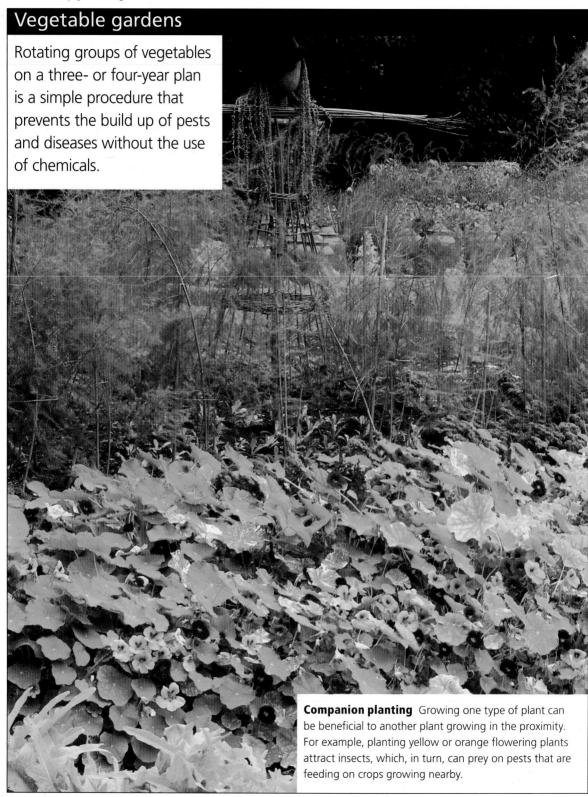

Companion planting Growing one type of plant can be beneficial to another plant growing in the proximity. For example, planting yellow or orange flowering plants attract insects, which, in turn, can prey on pests that are feeding on crops growing nearby.

Three-year crop rotation

The most common rotation is the three-year plan. Divide the plot into three sections and each year grow a different crop in each section, giving a two-year gap between each group of crops.

Crops are usually grouped into peas and beans, brassicas, and root vegetables as each of these groups have similar cultivation requirements. It also gives a chance for pests and diseases that are specific to a group of crops to die away. Crop rotation is of limited use for pathogens and pests that have a very broad host range and also for those that can survive for a very long time in the soil. If you have a large plot, a four-year plan is worthwhile where potatoes are planted as a fourth crop.

Strict rotation might be impractical in small areas and, if this is the case, grow wherever it is convenient. If problems are encountered, it is best to choose a new place for planting or grow in containers with sterile compost.

Year 1
The pea family includes peas, French beans, broad beans, and green manures, such as vetches and lupins. They require organic matter but little fertilizer. Their roots can fix nitrogen, which helps crops the following year. After harvest, cut down plants and leave roots to rot. Rotation helps to prevent diseases such as fusarium wilt and downy mildews and pests such as pea thrips.

Year 2
The brassica family includes Brussels sprouts, broccoli, cabbage, cauliflower, swede, turnip, radish, and rape. Brassicas need a fertile soil so they should follow peas and beans. They benefit from an alkaline soil, so check the pH (see p.14) and lime the soil if the pH is too low. Rotation will prevent diseases such as ring spot, white blister, downy mildews, and, to some extent, clubroot.

Year 3
Root crops include carrot, parsley, parsnip, and salsify, which need moderate fertilization. Rotation helps prevent diseases such as parsnip canker. Or plant tomatoes and potatoes in year three. They need lots of fertilizers and organic matter. Potatoes ensure the soil is well cultivated. Rotation reduces potato cyst eelworms, potato spraing, and powdery scab.

What are pests and diseases?

Garden plants are continually exposed to fungi, bacteria, viruses, insects, and many other creatures that have the potential to cause damage. Fortunately, a plant's natural defences are able to resist most attacks and the environment is not always favourable for them to occur in the first place. Recognizing symptoms and their distribution on the plant is very important in identifying the cause of the problem. Once that is known, it is much easier to see how to overcome the pest or disease.

Know your enemy: pests

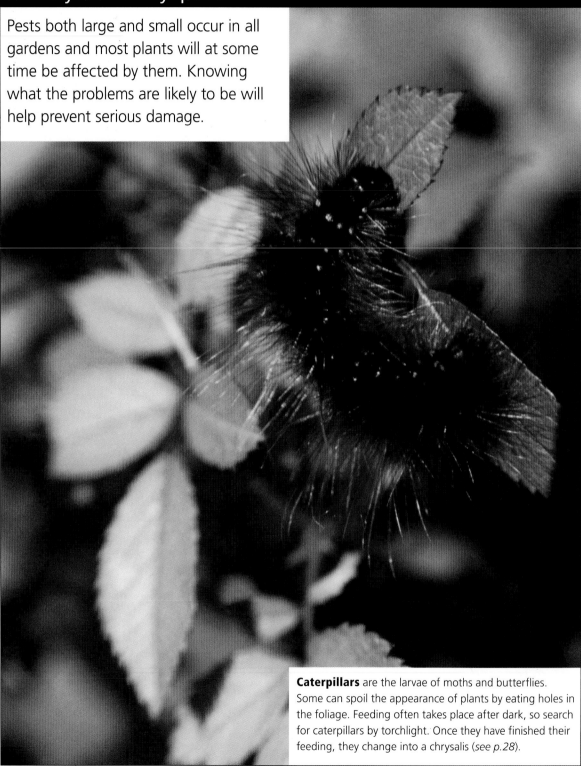

Pests both large and small occur in all gardens and most plants will at some time be affected by them. Knowing what the problems are likely to be will help prevent serious damage.

Caterpillars are the larvae of moths and butterflies. Some can spoil the appearance of plants by eating holes in the foliage. Feeding often takes place after dark, so search for caterpillars by torchlight. Once they have finished their feeding, they change into a chrysalis (*see p.28*).

All parts of a plant can be attacked by pests, from the roots to the shoot tips. Some pests are of microscopic size, such as nematodes or eelworms and some mites. Their identification therefore often depends on recognizing the symptoms they cause on plants. Other pests, such as birds and mammals, are easily seen. In between is a large array of smaller pests, such as insects, mites, woodlice, millipedes, slugs, and snails. Most are visible to the naked eye, but a hand lens is sometimes needed to see the smaller pests more clearly.

Pests damage plants in various ways. Insects, such as beetles, moth and butterfly caterpillars, sawflies, and earwigs, have biting mouthparts that they use to eat holes in foliage, flowers, fruits, and roots. Other insects, such as aphids, whitefly, mealybugs, scales, thrips, capsid bugs, and mites, have sucking mouthparts that they insert into plant tissues in order to feed on sap. Some insects, mites, and nematodes, cause plants to produce abnormal growths known as galls in which the gall-formers live and feed.

While most pests attack plants from the outside, there are some that feed internally, such as leaf miners, stem borers, and fruit pests – codling moth caterpillars, for example (*see p.122*).

Mammals and birds Squirrels, deer, rabbits, rats, and mice can cause serious damage to plants, as can pigeons and other pest birds. Other mammals, such as cats, dogs, and foxes, do not necessarily eat garden plants but can be a nuisance (*see pp.35–37*).

Above ground pests Caterpillars, sawfly larvae, beetles, earwigs, leaf miners, aphids, scale insects, leafhoppers, mealybugs, capsid bugs, thrips, and whitefly (*illustrated*) are examples of pests that feed on foliage, stems, flowers, and fruits. For more information, see pages 30–32.

Soil pests Cutworms, chafer grubs, vine weevil larvae (*illustrated*), leatherjackets, carrot fly, cabbage root fly, wireworms, and root aphids are all pests that live in the soil and feed on roots. Small plants may be killed or have their growth checked (*see pp.33 and 34*).

Pest lifecycles

Most pests start life as an egg, although some, such as aphids, give birth to live young. Between the egg and the adult stage, there is a period during which the immature nymphs or larvae feed and increase in size before finally becoming adults capable of reproduction, and so the cycle begins again.

Metamorphosis

Invertebrate animals can make the transition from egg to adult by two different processes. Some, such as slugs, snails, woodlice, earwigs, suckers, scale insects, mealybugs, whiteflies, aphids, thrips, and mites, undergo incomplete metamorphosis. The immature stages are not greatly different to the adult, except in size and lack of wings for the insects.

Complete metamorphosis occurs in butterflies and moths, beetles, flies, sawflies, and ants. Here the immature feeding stage is a caterpillar, grub, or maggot that is very different to the adult insect. When the larva has completed its feeding, it goes into a stage known as a pupa or chrysalis. During the pupal stage, the larval tissues break down and are reconstructed to form the adult insect.

The cabbage white butterfly is an insect that goes through complete metamorphosis, going from an egg to a caterpillar, to a pupa or chrysalis, before emerging as an adult butterfly. As with many pests with this lifecycle, it is the caterpillar or larval stage that causes the damage.

Cabbage white eggs
Batches of pale yellow eggs are laid on the underside of cabbage and other brassica leaves, with two generations occurring during the summer months.

Cabbage white caterpillar
The eggs hatch into yellow and black caterpillars that devour the leaves of their host plants. The caterpillars shed their outer skin five times as they grow larger.

Cabbage white pupa
When the caterpillar has completed its feeding, it crawls away to find a vertical surface that it can attach itself to and subsequently change into a chrysalis or pupa.

Surviving the winter

Pests can remain active throughout the year in greenhouses or on house plants, but most invertebrate garden pests go into a resting or dormant stage as temperatures fall and days get shorter in the autumn. They may overwinter as eggs, as immature nymphs and larvae, as pupae, or as adults. Those pests that overwinter as immature nymphs, larvae, or adults generally seek sheltered places in which to do so, such as in the soil, underneath loose bark, or in dense shrubby growth, such as conifer hedges.

In the spring, warmer weather brings plants back into growth and encourages pests out of their dormant phase. The hatching of aphid eggs on fruit trees and bushes, for example, is closely coordinated with the emergence of foliage from the buds. Both the eggs and the buds are responding to the same environmental conditions.

Earwig with eggs Earwigs overwinter as adult insects in the soil. The females lay their eggs in midwinter and remain with them until they hatch. The earwig is one of the few insects that show parental care for their eggs and young nymphs.

When pests thrive

Light infestations of pests have little impact, but as their numbers increase, the feeding pressure on garden plants becomes increasingly obvious. Plant growth may slow down, particularly where pests are feeding at the shoot tips and distorting the new growth. The foliage also becomes marked by holes where caterpillars and other pests have eaten parts of the leaves. Damage in late summer is of less significance because by then the growing season is coming to an end and so the consequences for the plant are less.

Population explosions

Small pests often have rapid reproductive rates that allow heavy infestations to develop quickly. Most pests are favoured by warm conditions and develop much more rapidly when temperatures are high. This may allow them to produce several generations during the summer. Predators, parasites, and diseases can keep pests at a low level, but if these natural controls are not operating, pests can breed unchecked. Sometimes the use of pesticides does more harm than good by eliminating the pest's natural enemies, giving the pest a free run.

Snails and slugs Most pests like it warm and dry but snails and slugs prefer cool damp conditions, which is why they do most of their feeding at night or after rain. These pests are particularly damaging to seedlings and soft young growth on herbaceous plants – for information on traps, see page 56.

Aphid outbreaks Greenfly and blackfly reproduce rapidly throughout the spring and summer months. The all-female populations of these pests shorten the lifecycle by giving birth to live young instead of laying eggs. This can result in plants becoming heavily infested in just a few weeks.

Above ground pests

Pests that feed above ground are easier to detect than those that live in the soil and the damage they cause is also more obvious. All above ground parts of plants, including the stem, foliage, flowers, and fruits or seeds, can be damaged by pests – and in many different ways, as shown here.

Some pests suck sap, which can result in stunted growth or distorted leaves. Other pests eat holes in the foliage and flowers, while yet others are internal feeders that tunnel through the stems, leaves, or fruits.

There are various other ways that pests can damage plants. For example, sap-sucking insects, such as some aphids, leafhoppers, and thrips, can spread plant virus diseases (see p.41) on their mouthparts when they move from plant to plant.

In addition, aphids, whitefly, mealybugs, and some scale insects excrete a sugary substance, called honeydew, which makes the foliage sticky. Black sooty moulds then often develop on the honeydew, causing further disfigurement to the plant. Other pests, particularly some insects and mites, induce abnormal growths known as galls (see p.68).

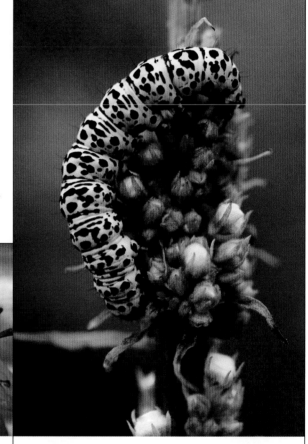

Ants
These familiar insects nest in the soil, but they climb plants to collect the sweet honeydew that aphids excrete. Ants cause little direct damage to plants, but they can be a nuisance and they inadvertently protect aphids by driving ladybirds away.

Beetles
There are many different beetle pests. Some, such as the lily beetle (see p.100), asparagus beetle (see p.121), and viburnum beetle (see p.81), eat foliage in both the adult and grub stages. With raspberry beetle (see p.128), it is the grub that damages the fruits.

Caterpillars
Caterpillars are the larval stage of butterflies and moths. Most species are not pests, but some have caterpillars that most distinctly are as they eat holes in leaves, bore into stems and fruits, and eat roots. Some of the smallest caterpillars feed within the leaves as leaf miners. Caterpillars can be distinguished from similar larvae of sawflies (see overleaf) by counting the clasping legs on the abdomen. Sawfly larvae have at least seven pairs, whereas butterfly and moth caterpillars have five or less. Control methods are given on pages 50–63; for specific hosts see pages 64–139.

Aphids

Also known as greenfly, blackfly, and plant lice, aphids suck sap from most garden plants using their needle-like mouthparts. Heavy infestations stunt growth and soil the plant with their sticky excrement – honeydew – and resulting sooty mould. For most of the spring and summer, aphids are wingless females that give birth to live young. When the aphids need to move on to another host plant, winged forms of the aphid develop. Many overwinter as eggs laid in the autumn on the branches of trees and shrubs. Control methods are given for specific hosts on pages 64–139.

Earwigs

Earwigs hide in dark places during the day. At night, they emerge to eat soft foliage and the petals of flowers, such as dahlia, chrysanthemum, and clematis (see p.84). In some years earwigs can be particularly abundant and damaging.

Cuckoo spit

This frothy white liquid is often seen in early summer on lavender (see p.131) and many other plants. It is secreted by a creamy white froghopper nymph that is sucking sap from the stems. Despite the spit's obvious presence, little real damage is caused to the plants.

Capsid bugs

These sap-sucking insects attack the shoot tips, flowers, buds, and fruits, especially apples (see p.122), killing cells in the developing leaves and blooms. This results in the expanding leaves tearing into many small holes, and flowers abort or open unevenly.

Leaf-cutting bees

The females cut pieces of leaf from the edges of roses and other plants. These are flown to the nest tunnel in dry soil, rotten wood, or a hollow plant stem and used to form cells in which larvae develop. The adult bees are pollinators so are best tolerated.

Above ground pests *continued*

Moths
Moths mainly fly at night, which is when they lay eggs on their host plants. It is the caterpillar stage that does the damage (*see p.30*). Some moth larvae are leaf miners. Control methods are given on pages 50–63; for specific hosts see pages 64–139.

Wasps
As well as inflicting painful stings, wasps cause damage to ripening fruits. These social insects live in communal nests that are headed by a queen wasp with several hundred worker wasps. Adult wasps eat other insects, some of which may be garden pests.

Sawflies
Sawflies have caterpillar-like larvae with seven or more pairs of clasping legs on their abdomens. Sawfly larvae often feed together in groups and can quickly devour the foliage of certain trees, shrubs, and herbaceous plants. When disturbed, they grip the leaf with the legs on their thorax and wave their abdomens, giving an S-shape to their bodies. Other sawfly pests feed as larvae inside developing fruits or as leaf miners. Adult sawflies do not damage plants. Control methods are given for specific hosts on pages 64–139.

Scale insects
Scales are sap-sucking insects that infest the stems and foliage of many plants. Some produce a sugary excrement, known as honeydew, that makes plants sticky and allows the growth of sooty moulds. The soft-bodied insects are covered by shells or scales. When mature, some scale insects deposit their eggs beneath their shells, but others, such as cushion scales, secrete a white waxy material in which the eggs are embedded. These egg masses are often more visible than the scale itself. Control methods are given for specific hosts on pages 64–139.

Leaf miners
Most leaf miners are fly or moth larvae, but there are some leaf-mining sawflies and beetles. They make distinctive discoloured lines or blotches in the foliage where they have been eating the tissues. Control methods are given for specific hosts on pages 64–139.

Virus vectors
It is mainly sap-sucking insects that transmit virus diseases when they move from one plant to another. Aphids, leafhoppers, and thrips are often responsible, but some soil-dwelling nematodes also spread virus diseases, especially on soft fruit.

Soil and root-dwelling pests

Soil-dwelling pests are mostly hidden from view but can have a severe effect on plants because a healthy root system is essential for good growth.

Soil pests range in size from microscopic nematodes or eelworms to insects, millipedes, woodlice, and slugs that can be readily seen with the naked eye. If a large proportion of the root system is damaged, plants can be killed, especially if the damage occurs when the plant is still at an early stage of its growth. Root vegetables, such as carrots and turnips, can survive attacks by root fly larvae, but the plants are made unfit for human consumption by the damage.

Some creatures found in the soil, such as millipedes and woodlice, feed mainly on decaying plant material. They may nibble seedlings but they are unlikely to harm established plants.

Soil-dwelling pests are often difficult to control because of their hidden nature and a lack of suitable pesticides for use in this situation.

Root aphids
Root aphids live underground and suck sap from the roots and the base of stems on plants such as lettuce, beans, carrots, auricula (*pictured*), and other ornamental plants. Infested plants lack vigour and tend to wilt in sunny weather. Control is difficult; on edible plants, crop rotation (*see p.23*) may help.

Wireworms
Wireworms grow up to 25mm (1in) long and have rather stiff, yellowish orange bodies. They are the larval stage of click beetles, but only the larval stage causes damage. They can kill seedling plants and bore into potato tubers, root vegetables, and onion bulbs. Large numbers of wireworms live in grassland, where they cause no noticeable damage. However, the first year or two of cultivation on a newly dug plot can see heavy damage to vegetables growing on the site. There is no insecticide available for their control in gardens.

Vine weevil grubs
The creamy white, legless grubs of vine weevils are mainly a problem on plants grown in pots or other containers, but also occur in open ground. They are fully grown as larvae in autumn to spring, which is when plants can be killed. Control methods are on page 138.

Chafer grubs
Larger than vine weevil grubs, these pests have three pairs of legs at the head end, curved bodies. and as adults are beetles. They eat grass roots and can kill small ornamental plants and vegetables. Control methods are given on page 104.

Invertebrate pests

Invertebrate pests are small creatures without backbones, such as nematodes or eelworms, slugs and snails, insects, mites, millipedes, and woodlice. Many are not garden pests, but a minority can cause problems.

Gardens and greenhouses are home to a wide range of invertebrate animals. Some are welcome as pollinators, predators, and parasites of pests, or as recyclers of dead plant materials. Many others live and feed in gardens without being either beneficial to gardeners or causing problems through damaging plants. The minority that are pests soon make their presence felt by the adverse effects they have on plant growth and appearance.

All parts of a plant are potentially at risk from these predators. Most of the damage is seen on the foliage and flowers, but there are unseen pests that feed on roots or inside the stems and fruits.

Some examples of different types of the invertebrate animals that are more commonly found in gardens are shown on this page.

Slugs and snails

Snails differ from slugs in having a shell into which they can withdraw their bodies. Both types of mollusc secrete a slimy substance from their bodies and this can leave a silvery trail where they have moved over a plant. They feed by rasping the surface of leaves, stems, and flowers with their "tongues". Non-chemical treatments for slugs and snails are given on pages 56, 58–59, and 63, and see also using pellets on page 53.

Mites

Most mites have four pairs of legs when adult. Gall mites have only two pairs. Some, such as gall mites, induce abnormal growths. Control methods are given for specific hosts on pages 64–139.

Woodlice

Woodlice are terrestrial crustaceans that hide during the day in dark, damp places. At night they feed mainly on decaying plant material but can damage seedlings or enlarge damage started by other pests.

Millipedes

Millipedes are often found with woodlice and have similar feeding habits. They have elongate segmented bodies, with two pairs of legs on each segment. There is no insecticidal control for these invertebrates.

Insects

Adult insects have segmented bodies with three pairs of legs and, in most species, two pairs of wings on the thorax. They include beetles, flies, moths, sawflies, thrips, aphids, and whitefly.

Mammals and birds

Birds and mammals are less abundant than the smaller garden pests, but they have bigger appetites and some can be a nuisance in the garden, even if they are not eating the plants.

Birds and mammals can be some of the most difficult problems that gardeners have to contend with. In most cases, it is not feasible to kill these animals, even where it is legal to do so. Netting or fencing can be effective in protecting plants (*see pp.58–59*) from some of these pests, but it can be expensive and may detract from the appearance of your garden.

Various repellent substances and scaring devices are available (*see also pp.58–59*), but generally do not give effective long-term protection. Repellent substances rely on unpleasant smells or tastes; frequent applications are often needed to maintain protection. Scaring devices range from scarecrows to devices that emit ultrasonic sound. These can be effective when newly installed, but birds and mammals get used to them after a while. With problem birds and mammals, it is a matter of sharing the garden and trying to reduce any damage caused.

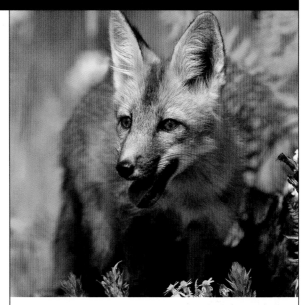

Foxes
Increasingly common in urban areas, foxes damage lawns in search of chafer grubs (*see p.33*) and foul gardens with their faeces and strong-smelling urine. They will dig up new plantings, especially where bonemeal or dried blood has been used. Foxes sometimes dig dens under garden sheds where they raise their cubs in early summer.

Cats and dogs
The main problem with cats and dogs is their faeces, which can get underfoot and create an unpleasant smell. Their urine can scorch plants, especially when female dogs urinate on lawns. Cats are often the bigger problem as they roam more freely into gardens than dogs. They are attracted to areas of soft dry ground when looking for somewhere to defaecate. This problem with cats can be reduced by planting densely to deny them open ground.

Badgers
Badgers rip up lawns in search of chafer grubs from autumn to spring and eat carrots, parsnips, and sweet corn from vegetable patches. They also use gardens as latrines and dig a series of shallow holes containing their droppings. It is not possible to exclude these powerful and persistent animals with ordinary netting or fencing, as they will push it aside or dig underneath, but electric fencing can be effective.

Mammals and birds *continued*

Mice and rats

Mice eat the seeds of germinating sweetcorn, peas, and beans. They also eat crocus corms and orchard fruits, both in gardens and when produce is being stored in sheds. They can be controlled by setting mouse traps. If traps are set in gardens, place them under log or brick shelters to reduce the danger to birds. Rats cause similar damage to mice and can also damage root vegetables. They can carry Weil's disease in their urine and so are a particular problem in food stores. They can be controlled by trapping or with poison baits.

Moles

Moles burrow through the soil and patrol their tunnels in search of earthworms and insect grubs. While creating the tunnel system, moles deposit heaps of excavated soil on the surface. This interferes with mowing on lawns and results in an uneven surface when tunnels collapse. Seedlings and low-growing plants can be buried by molehills in flower beds and vegetable plots. Moles can be controlled by trapping (*see p.57*). Ultrasonic sound devices are available for scaring moles away, but they are not always effective.

Deer

Destructive pests in gardens, deer eat the foliage and shoot tips from many plants. The males also rub their antlers against tree trunks, causing damage to the bark and side shoots, which can kill young trees. A robust fence is needed to keep deer out of a garden. There are some plants that are less likely to be eaten, although even these can be damaged when newly planted. Daffodils, hydrangeas, and delphiniums usually escape damage, as do tough-leaved plants, such as *Yucca* and *Cordyline*. Deer are inquisitive feeders that are attracted to new plantings.

Rabbits

Many vegetables and herbaceous plants are grazed by rabbits. They also kill trees and shrubs by gnawing bark from the stems, particularly during winter. Protect new plantings with wire netting or cloches (*see p.58*) and put tree guards around the base of young trees. If rabbits are a persistent problem, enclose the garden with a rabbit-proof wire netting of 2.5cm (1in) mesh. This needs to be 1.4m (4½ft) high with the bottom 30cm (12in) of the mesh bent outwards on the soil surface to stop rabbits burrowing underneath.

Squirrels

Introduced from North America, the grey squirrel has largely replaced the native red squirrel in Britain. It eats fruits, nuts, sweetcorn, flower buds, tulip bulbs, and crocus corms. The most destructive form of damage that the squirrel is capable of is bark stripping on trees. Where most of the bark has been lost from the trunk circumference, growth above that point dries up and dies. Squirrels can be trapped but control is ultimately unlikely to be effective unless it is carried out over a much wider area than the size of the average garden.

Pigeons

The wood pigeon is mainly a problem in vegetable gardens where they devour the foliage of peas, cabbages, and other brassicas. Damage can occur at any time of year, but often increases in the winter. Pigeons can be shot, but this is not usually possible in gardens. Growing vulnerable vegetables under netting will keep pigeons away from the foliage (*see p.59*). Scaring devices, such as imitation hawks, humming tapes, scarecrows, and glitter strips are likely to give only temporary protection against the ravages of this bird.

Herons

Herons are not numerous birds but they cover a wide area in their search for food. They soon learn where garden ponds are located and will land to take fish, frogs, and other pond wildlife. Netting is effective in protecting ponds against these birds, especially those that contain valuable ornamental fish, such as koi carp. A model heron placed at the pond margin is sometimes recommended as a deterrent on the grounds that herons normally prefer to feed alone. This, however, is not a reliable means of protection.

Know your enemy: diseases

Diseases are sicknesses of plants caused by microorganisms known as pathogens, which are most commonly fungi, bacteria, and viruses. The majority of diseases are caused by fungi.

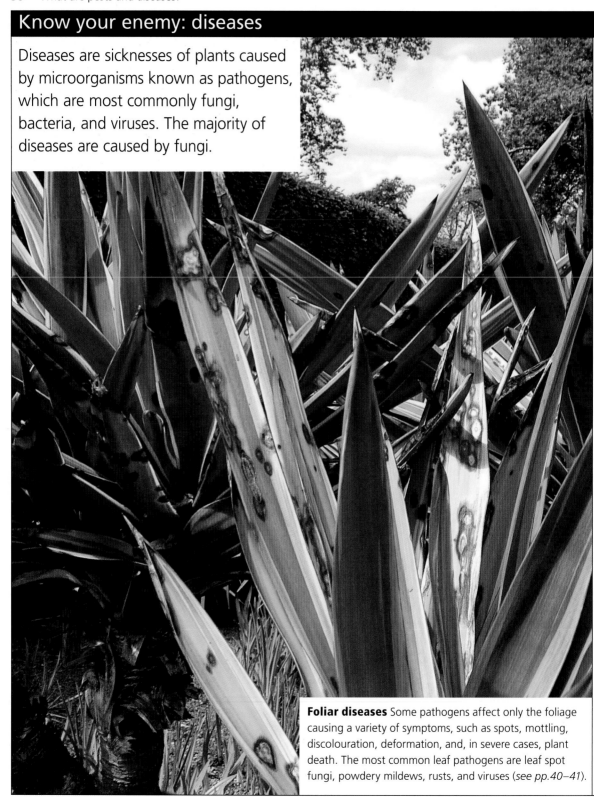

Foliar diseases Some pathogens affect only the foliage causing a variety of symptoms, such as spots, mottling, discolouration, deformation, and, in severe cases, plant death. The most common leaf pathogens are leaf spot fungi, powdery mildews, rusts, and viruses (*see pp.40–41*).

A serious disease is a rare event and to occur it needs a susceptible host, a virulent pathogen, and a favourable environment. Leaf spots fungi, powdery mildews, and rusts are airborne and spread via spores on air currents or water splashing. Wood decay fungi spread by releasing airborne spores from their brackets or toadstools. They also spread by root contact. Honey fungus is unusual because most of the spread is not by spores but by root contact or by rhizomorphs (bootlaces), a structure it produces to travel from tree to tree in the soil.

Fungi-like organisms such as *Pythium* and *Phytophthora* produce infective spores that spread in the soil through the water flow. They can also form resting spores that remain dormant in the soil in the absence of a susceptible host. Some species can also produce airborne spores causing leaf blight, twig die-back, and bleeding cankers on susceptible hosts.

Bacteria survive in soil and plant debris. They invade mainly through wounds and are splashed from the soil to the leaves. They spread rapidly in wet weather. Viruses rely on vectoring by insects, nematodes, or mechanical damage to pass them on to new hosts. They may also be seed-borne.

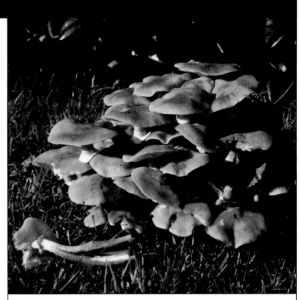

Fungi Many different fungi cause the decay of roots or stem base, or branches and stems. They produce annual or perennial fruiting structures, such as toadstools or brackets, most frequently in the autumn. The biggest threat to trees and shrubs is honey fungus.

Rots Root and stem rots can be caused by a variety of pathogens, commonly *Phytophthora* (see p.42). Affected plants become less vigorous, a tree canopy thins and die-back is widespread, and the root system is reduced and looks brown or black with no obvious fungal growth.

Wilts These diseases are caused by fungi or bacteria that block the vascular tissues resulting in wilting, stunting, discolouration, stem die-back, or death. The most common wilt diseases are caused by fungi such as *Verticillium* and *Fusarium* (see p.43).

Foliar diseases

A number of diseases only affect aerial parts of plants. Some of them, such as downy mildews, can severely affect a plant's health, while others, such as many leaf spots, only spoil its appearance.

Some pathogens, such as rusts and powdery mildews, are easily recognisable because of their typical growth on the leaf surfaces. Others are much more difficult to confirm because of their microscopic size and the symptoms they produce are not always diagnostic. For example, distortion and stunting caused by many viruses can easily be confused with weedkiller damage and fungal leaf spots can sometimes be confused with environmental damage. As the number of chemical remedies is limited for the amateur gardener, cultural techniques are key to avoiding the spread of the diseases. Among these are:

- Remove infected plants or parts promptly.
- Avoid overhead irrigation.
- Keep plants adequately watered, fed, and mulched.
- Remove fallen material at the end of the season.

Fungal leaf spots
Most leaf spots are produced by fungi, but some are caused by bacteria or unsuitable growing conditions. Leaf spot fungi and bacteria thrive in moist weather. Some attack a range of plants, others are host specific. Spots vary in size, shape, and colour. They can be disfiguring but are unlikely to kill plants. Most fungi survive unfavourable periods. To control, follow the techniques described (*left*) or specific treatments, where available, on pages 64–139.

Downy mildews
These are fungi-like organisms that can affect many plants, but are usually genus specific. Off-white mould forms on the underside of leaves, which may be vein-delineated, with corresponding yellow blotches on the upper leaf. Remove diseased plants, improve air circulation and avoid overhead watering. Lettuce downy mildew can be protected against with the fungicide mancozeb. Resting spores can persist in soil for years.

Powdery mildews
Powdery mildews include many fungal species that affect a very wide range of plants, but each usually only infect a group of related plants. Typically, a powdery white coating appears on any part of the plant and infected tissue becomes distorted. The leaves may drop, buds die, or stems die back. Watering during dry periods and improving air circulation by pruning or ventilation will help, as does spraying with an appropriate fungicide.

Viruses

Plants exhibit a range of symptoms when infected by viruses, the most common being chlorotic patches on leaves, often in the forms of mosaics, ringspots, and mottles. Necrotic patches can also result. An infected plant may appear stunted. Viruses are often present in plants propagated from a portion of another plant, such as dahlias and cannas. Transmission is normally by insect vectors or sap. Some are highly contagious and spread by contact between a plant and a surface on which virus particles are present. Viruses cannot be cured so destroy affected plants.

Rusts

Pustules of powdery orange/brown spores appear on the undersides of leaves and stems with corresponding pale spots on the upper surface. Often leaves fall prematurely. Fungicides are available.

Foliar scabs

Dark green patches appear on the leaves leading to dead tissues and premature leaf fall. The infections also show as dark sunken spots on fruits or berries, or stem die-back. Treatments are given on pages 64–139.

Smuts

Most smuts are noted by powdery black masses of spores. Leaf spots appear and organs distort. Smuts produce resilient spores that can persist in the soil for several years. Controls are described on pages 64–139.

Grey mould

The grey mould fungus is very common and affects many plants. It is mainly associated with stem and leaf rots and spreads rapidly by air-borne spores, especially in wet conditions (*see p.136*).

Rots and wilts

Diseases that cause symptoms of wilt, stem decay, and root rots are considered in this section. These are destructive pathogens often leading to plant death.

The most common root pathogens in gardens are honey fungus and *Phytophthora*. Thorough root examination is often essential to confirm them. Above ground, both pathogens would lead to widespread die-back and collapse of the plant.

Distribution of symptoms may also give some clues as to which disease is causing problems in the garden. For example, partial die-back as opposed to overall die-back is often due to a wilt disease rather than a root rot pathogen. The appearance of bracket fungi can also indicate other wood decay pathogens.

As there are no soil sterilants or chemicals available for gardeners to treat these problems, sanitation is important in managing these diseases. Knowing exactly which pathogen has killed your plants helps when choosing suitable resistant replacement plants.

Sclerotinia

Symptoms of *Sclerotinia* include sudden wilting, yellowing of basal leaves, and a brown rot of the stem. This is associated with abundant white mould, often containing hard, black structures called sclerotia. Infected plant material should be destroyed before the sclerotia are released into the soil because they may survive in the ground for many years. For this reason, do not compost the infected plants either. Susceptible plants should not be grown there for up to eight years. The potential host range for this disease is very wide.

Phytophthora

Phytophthora is a microscopic fungus-like organism. There are many species of it, some of which are highly specific, while others have a wide host range. Infected plants most commonly suffer from a root or stem rot, but sometimes have twig and leaf blight. The disease may be associated with bleeding cankers. As result, branches die back. The disease is encouraged by wet conditions. *Phytophthora* can remain dormant in the soil for years. Remove affected plants and the surrounding soil. Improve drainage and keep the infected area free of woody plants for three years.

Verticillium wilt

This wilt disease affects a broad range of edibles and ornamentals. Symptoms of Verticillium wilt include individual branches wilting and eventually dying back, often over successive years. Typically, within the vascular tissue of these branches dark streaking is evident. Applying an ammonium-based fertilizer to the root spread may encourage the subsequent production of a new ring of disease-free vascular tissue. The fungus *Verticillium* is soil-borne, so the best treatment is to remove badly affected plants and to subsequently replace them with resistant species.

Honey fungus

Honey fungus causes a fatal disease that can affect all woody plants. Symptoms include thinning of the canopy, branch die-back, or the sudden death of a plant. A white sheet of fungal mycelium will be present between the bark and wood. Sometimes, honey coloured mushrooms with white gills and a collar on the stipe may appear in autumn. Destroy infected plants, taking care to remove as much of their root system as possible. Choose plants that are less susceptible to infection, such as *Acer negundo*, beech, box, ivy, laurel, sweet chestnut, and yew.

Fusarium wilt

This fungal disease can affect many herbaceous plants and vegetables. Plants wilt, older leaves look scorched, a section of stem base reveals a dark discolouration of the tissues. The fungus persists in the soil or in plant debris. Remove infected plants and surrounding soil.

Silver leaf

This fungal disease often affects trees, especially *Prunus*. The leaves become silver, branches die back, and small purple bracket fungi may appear on dead wood. Cutting dying branches in the summer to below where staining ends can save the tree.

Quick diagnosis of the most common symptoms

Listed here are symptoms of the most common pests and diseases described in this book, divided into the plant parts that are most likely to be affected. Bear in mind that some pests and diseases present more than one symptom.

If you can't find what you are looking for on pages 44–49, but know what your plant is, refer to the specific group, such as roses on pages 86–87, *Prunus* on pages 124–125, and potatoes on pages 116–117, or check the index. Sometimes a disease or pest relating to one specific plant will also attack other plants. For example, hollyhock rust attacks hollyhocks (*Althaea rosea*), but also lavatera and other related genera. Lists of any such plants are given at the start of their relative section.

Leaves
Symptoms: Leaf spots generally round and spreading over leaf veins; also elongate spots on stems
Potential diseases: Fungal leaf spots (*p.40*)
See the following:
Arbutus leaf spots (*p.70*)
Brassica dark and light leaf spots (*p.114*)
Brassica ring spot (*p.114*)
Celery leaf spot (*p.121*)

Cherry leaf scorch (*p.124*)
Cherry leaf spot (*p.124*)
Currant and gooseberry leaf spot (*p.126*)
Dahlia smut (*p.103*)
Escallonia leaf spots (*p.77*)
Hellebore leaf blotch (*p.96*)
Iris leaf spot (*p.101*)
Ivy leaf spot (*p.84*)
Lily disease (*p.100*)
Mulberry leaf spot (*p.127*)
Pansy leaf spots (*p.99*)
Rhododendron leaf spot (*p.83*)
Robinia decline (*p.74*)
Rose black spot (*p.87*)
Strawberry leaf spot (*p.129*)
Tar spot of Acer (*p.70*)
Yucca leaf spot (*p.81*)

Symptoms: Spots often angular because they are limited by leaf veins; colour is usually uniform; spots may initially be water soaked
Potential pest/disease: Leaf and bud eelworms, bacterial leaf spots
See the following:
Bean halo blight (*p.113*)
Delphinium black blotch (*p.95*)

Leaf and bud eelworms (*p.91*)
Mulberry bacterial blight (*p.127*)

Symptoms: Irregular brown/black spots or blotches on the leaves; spots may coalesce and leaves fall prematurely; branches or stems may die back
Potential disease: Leaf blight
See the following:
Bean anthracnose (*p.113*)
Bean chocolate spot (*p.113*)
Box blight (*p.80*)
Dogwood anthracnose (*p.71*)
Holly leaf blight (*p.77*)
Holly leaf miner (*p.76*)
Horse chestnut leaf blotch (*p.72*)
Leek white tip (*p.120*)
Lupin anthracnose (*p.94*)
Peony wilt (*p.96*)
Plane anthracnose (*p.74*)
Potato and tomato blight (*p.117 and p.119*)
Quince leaf blight (*p.74*)
Rhododendron leaf blight and die-back (*p.83*)
Willow anthracnose (*p.75*)
Willow black canker (*p.75*)

Tar spot of Acer

Hellebore leaf blotch

Rhododendron leaf blight and die-back

Symptoms: Blackish brown discoloured areas, often sharply divided from uninfested parts by larger leaf veins
Potential pest: Leaf and bud eelworm (*p.91*)

Symptoms: Fine, pale mottling on the upper surface, which gradually becomes yellowish brown
Potential pests: Leafhoppers, red spider mites, thrips
See the following:
Conifer red spider mite (*p.76*)
Fruit tree red spider mite (*p.111*)
Gladiolus thrips (*p.100*)
Glasshouse leafhopper (*p.138*)
Glasshouse red spider mite (*p.136*)
Glasshouse thrips (*p.137*)
Pea thrips (*p.112*)
Pieris lacebug (*p.80*)
Privet thrips (*p.76*)
Rose leafhopper (*p.87*)
Sage leafhopper (*p.130*)

Symptoms: Dark green patches on tree leaves leading to dead tissue and premature leaf fall
Potential disease: Tree scabs (*p.69*)
See the following:
Apple and pear scabs (*p.69*)

Symptoms: Chlorotic patches, often appearing in the form of mosaics, ringspots, and mottles; distortion of leaves
Potential disease: Viruses (*p.41*)
See the following:
Camellia yellow mottle virus (*p.82*)
Canna viruses (*p.97*)
Cucumber mosaic virus (*p.119*)
Glasshouse viruses (*p.139*)
Hellebore black death (*p.96*)
Lettuce viruses (*p.118*)
Nicotiana viruses (*p.99*)
Orchid viruses (*p.139*)
Parsnip viruses (*p.117*)
Passion flower viruses (*p.85*)
Petunia viruses (*p.99*)
Raspberry leaf and bud mite (*p.128*)
Rose viruses (*p.87*)
Strawberry viruses (*p.129*)
Tomato viruses (*p.119*)

Symptoms: Leaves are distorted and filled with powdery black masses of spores
Potential disease: Smuts (*p.41*)
See the following:
Anemone smut (*p.101*)

Symptoms: Off-white mould on the underside of leaves and corresponding yellow, purple, or brown blotches on the upper leaves
Potential disease: Downy mildew (*p.40*)

See the following:
Brassica downy mildew (*p.114*)
Grape erinose mite (*p.127*)
Hebe downy mildew (*p.81*)
Impatiens downy mildew (*p.98*)
Lettuce downy mildew (*p.118*)
Nicotiana downy mildew (*p.99*)
Pansy downy mildew (*p.99*)
Pea downy mildew (*p.112*)

Symptoms: Powdery white coating with infected tissue becoming distorted and leaves may drop
Potential disease: Powdery mildew (*p.40*)
See the following:
Acanthus powdery mildew (*p.96*)
American gooseberry mildew (*p.127*)
Bay powdery mildew (*p.130*)
Cucumber powdery mildew (*p.119*)
Delphinium powdery mildew (*p.95*)
Geranium powdery mildew (*p.94*)
Honeysuckle powdery mildew (*p.85*)
Oak powdery mildew (*p.73*)
Pea powdery mildew (*p.112*)
Raspberry powdery mildew (*p.128*)
Rhododendron powdery mildew (*p.83*)
Sweet pea powdery mildew (*p.98*)

Rose leafhopper

Camellia yellow mottle virus

Acanthus powdery mildew

Quick diagnosis of the most common symptoms *continued*

Leaves *continued*

Symptoms: White waxy bands of eggs on the underside of evergreen leaves, often with heavy coating of sooty mould on upper leaf surface
Potential pest: Cushion scale (*p.66*)

Symptom: White waxy clusters on glasshouse plants
Potential pests: Fluted scale (*p.137*), mealybug (*p.138*)
See the following:
Phormium mealybug (*p.92*)

Symptom: White chalky eruptions on the underside of leaves
Potential disease: White blister (*p.109*)

Symptoms: Soft-bodied insects covered by shells or scales; foliage sometimes sticky, with growth of sooty moulds
Potential pest: Scale insects (*p.32*)
See the following:
Brown scale (*p.110*)
Cushion scale (*p.66*)
Euonymus scale (*p.80*)
Fluted scale (*p.137*)
Hemispherical scale (*p.137*)
Horse chestnut scale (*p.72*)
Hydrangea scale (*p.80*)
Oleander scale (*p.137*)
Soft scale (*p.137*)
Wisteria scale (*p.85*)

Symptoms: Abnormal growths or galls on foliage
Potential cause: Various pests or fungi
See the following:
Acer pimple gall (*p.70*)
Azalea and camellia galls (*p.82*)
Bay sucker (*p.130*)
Box sucker (*p.80*)
Elm gall mite (*p.71*)
Eucalyptus gall wasp (*p.71*)
Gall mites (*p.66*)
Gleditsia gall midge (*p.78*)
Lime nail gall mite (*p.72*)
Oak gall wasps (*p.73*)
Peach leaf curl (*p.124*)
Plum gall mite (*p.125*)
Violet gall midge (*p.93*)
Walnut gall mite (*p.74*)
Willow bean gall sawfly (*p.75*)

Symptoms: Pustules of powdery yellow/orange/brown/off-white spores on the undersides of leaves with corresponding pale spots on the upper surface; often leaves fall prematurely
Potential disease: Rust (*p.41*)
See the following:
Antirrhinum rust (*p.97*)
Bean rust (*p.113*)
Chrysanthemum brown rust (*p.95*)
Chrysanthemum white rust (*p.95*)
Fuchsia rust (*p.79*)
Hollyhock rust (*p.97*)

Iris rust (*p.101*), or black slit-like pustules
Mahonia rust (*p.81*)
Mint rust (*p.131*)
Pear rust (*p.123*)
Pelargonium rust (*p.94*)
Periwinkle rust (*p.97*)
Raspberry rust (*p.129*)
Rhododendron rust (*p.83*)
Rose rust (*p.87*)

Symptoms: Leaves turn silver and branches die back
Potential disease: Silver leaf disease (*p.43*)

Symptom: Twisting white or brown lines or mines causing brown, dried-up blotches in the leaves
Potential pest: Leaf miners (*p.32*)
See the following:
Allium leaf miner (*p.120*)
Apple leaf-mining moth (*p.122*)
Beet leaf miner (*p.121*)
Celery leaf miner (*p.121*)
Chrysanthemum leaf miner (*p.95*)
Holly leaf miner (*p.76*)
Holm oak leaf miner (*p.73*)
Horse chestnut leaf-mining moth (*p.72*)
Laburnum leaf miner (*p.78*)
Leek moth (*p.120*)
Lilac leaf miner (*p.78*)
Pyracantha leaf miner (*p.79*)
Sempervivum leaf miner (*p.92*)

Cushion scale   Oak gall wasps   Pear rust

Symptom: Foliage being eaten
Potential pests: Beetles (*p.30*), butterfly, moth, and sawfly larvae (*p.32*), mammals (*pp.35–7*), slugs and snails (*p.34*)
See the following:
Asparagus beetle (*p.121*)
Berberis sawfly (*p.78*)
Brassica flea beetles (*p.114*)
Cabbage white butterflies (*pp.98, 115*)
Colorado beetle (*p.108*)
Cotoneaster webber moth (*p.79*)
Elephant hawk moth (*p.79*)
Figwort weevil (*p.79*)
Geranium sawfly (*p.94*)
Geum sawfly (*p.93*)
Gooseberry sawflies (*p.127*)
Iris sawfly (*p.101*)
Lily beetle (*p.100*)
Mint beetle (*p.131*)
Mullein moth (*p.92*)
Oak processionary moth (*p.73*)
Pea and bean weevil (*p.112*)
Pear and cherry slugworm (*p.123*)
Rose slugworm sawfly (*p.86*)
Rosemary beetle (*p.130*)
Solomon's seal sawfly (*p.92*)
Tomato moth (*p.118*)
Tortrix moth (*p.90*; glasshouse *p.138*)
Viburnum beetle (*p.81*)
Vine weevil – adults (*p.34*)
Water lily beetle (*p.93*)
Willow leaf beetle (*p.75*)
Winter moth (*p.110*)

Symptom: Regular-sized pieces of leaf missing with smooth outline
Potential pest: Leaf-cutting bee (*p.31*)

Symptom: Holes on leaves on Prunus
Potential diseases: Bacterial canker (*p.124*), bacterial leaf spots, cherry leaf spot (*p.124*), fungal leaf spots (*p.40*)

Symptoms: Sudden wilting of the leaves, yellowing of basal leaves, a brown rot of the stem and abundant white mould
Potential disease: *Sclerotinia* (*p.42*)

Symptoms: Leaves wilt and stems die back; staining may or may not be visible in the stem tissues while roots are initially alive
Potential diseases: Wilts
See the following:
Clematis wilt (*p.84*)
Dutch elm disease (*p.71*)
Fusarium wilt (*p.43*)
Verticillium wilt (*p.43*)

Symptoms: Leaves wilt and die; stems die back; no staining is visible in the stem tissues, but roots are rotted
Potential diseases: Root rots
See the following:
Damping off (*p.139*)
Honey fungus (*p.43*)

Pansy sickness (*p.99*)
Phytophthora root rot (*p.42*)
Wisteria die-back (*p.85*)

Symptoms: Leaves wilt on hot days, recovering over night
Potential problems: Clubroot (*p.109*), root aphids (*p.33*)
See the following:
Lettuce root aphid (*p.118*)
Root mealybugs (*p.138*)

Symptoms: Tree leaves wilt and turn brown but remain attached to tree
Potential diseases: Cherry leaf scorch (*p.124*), Fireblight (*p.111*)

Symptoms: Dense colony of variously coloured sap-sucking insects on shoot tips and leaves, excreting a sticky honeydew
Potential pests: Aphids (see *p.31*), suckers, whitefly
See the following:
Beech woolly aphid (*p.70*)
Black bean aphid (*p.113*)
Cabbage whitefly (*p.115*)
Cherry blackfly (*p.124*)
Currant blister aphid (*p.126*)
Cypress aphid (*p.76*)
Eucalyptus sucker (*p.71*)
Glasshouse aphids (*p.139*)
Glasshouse whitefly (*p.136*)
(*continued overleaf*)

Rose slugworm sawfly

Sclerotinia

Glasshouse whitefly

Quick diagnosis of the most common symptoms *continued*

Leaves *continued*
Honeysuckle aphid (*p.85*)
Lupin aphid (*p.94*)
Mealy cabbage aphid (*p.115*)
Mealy plum aphid (*p.125*)
Pear bedstraw aphid (*p.123*)
Plum leaf-curling aphid (*p.125*)
Rose aphid (*p.86*)
Viburnum whitefly (*p.81*)
Water lily aphid (*p.93*)

Flowers and buds
Symptoms: Colour breaking
Potential disease: Virus (*p.41*)
See the following:
Petunia viruses (*p.99*)
Camellia yellow mottle virus (*p.82*)

Symptom: Flowers and/or buds with fluffy grey mould growth
Potential disease: Grey mould (*p.136*)
See the following:
Lily disease (*p.100*)

Symptoms: Anthers become swollen and distorted and are covered with masses of black spores
Potential disease: Smuts (*p.41*)
See the following:
Dianthus smut (*p.95*)

Symptom: Flowers aborting or open unevenly

Potential pest: Capsid bug (*p.31*)
Michaelmas daisy mite (*p.93*)

Symptom: Fruit tree flowers wilt and turn brown
Potential disease: Blossom wilt (*p.111*)

Symptom: Abnormal growths or galls on buds
Potential pests: Gall midges, gall mites (*p.66*)
See the following:
Blackcurrant big bud mites (*p.126*)
Broom gall mite (*p.78*)
Hemerocallis gall midge (*p.94*)

Symptom: Flower buds devoured on fruit trees and bushes
Potential pest: Birds (*p.111*)

Fruit
Symptoms: Dark blotches or spots on fruits and berries
Potential disease: Tree scabs (*p.69*)
See the following:
Quince leaf blight (*p.74*)

Symptom: Rings of buff spores on fruits
Potential disease: Brown rot (*p.123*)

Symptoms: Fruits with fluffy grey mould growth or with small white

rings sometimes associated with grey mould growth
Potential disease: Grey mould (*p.136*)
See the following:
Tomato ghost spot (*p.118*)
Strawberry grey mould (*p.129*)

Symptoms: Fruits with a white or off-white fungal coating
Potential disease: Powdery mildew (*p.40*)
See the following:
American gooseberry mildew (*p.127*)

See also fruit trees (*pp.122–125*), soft fruit (*pp.126–127*), and raspberries and strawberries (*pp.128–129*)

Trunks, branches, and stems
Symptom: Abnormal twig proliferation leading to reduction in flowering
Potential disease: Witches' broom (*p.68*)

Symptom: Dead sections on branches, main trunks, or stems
Potential diseases: Blossom wilt (*p.111*), cankers (*p.68*), fireblight (*p.111*)

Dianthus smut

Brown rot

Witches' broom

See the following:
Apple and pear canker (*p.123*)
Bacterial canker (*p.124*)
Poplar canker (*p.75*)
Rose canker and die-back (*p.87*)

Symptoms: Branches dying as a result of root or stem rot; fungal growth may or may not be apparent on dying stems or roots
Potential diseases: Coral spot (*p.67*), grey mould (*p.41*), honey fungus (*p.43*), *Phytophthora* (*p.42*), *Sclerotinia* (*p.42*), wood decay fungi (*p.69*)
See the following:
Lavender grey mould (*p.131*)
Peony wilt (*p.96*)
Robinia decline (*p.74*)
Roses (*p.86*)
Snowdrop grey mould (*p.103*)
Strawberry grey mould (*p.129*)
Tulip fire (*p.103*)
Wisteria die-back (*p.85*)
Yew Phytophthora root rot (*p.77*)

Symptom: Bleeding on stems or branches
Potential diseases: Cankers (*p.68*), root rots
See the following:
Bacterial canker (*p.124*)
Coryneum canker (*p.68*)
Honey fungus (*p.43*)

Horse chestnut bleeding canker (*p.72*)
Phytophthora (*p.42*)

Symptoms: Branches wilt and eventually die back; staining is visible in the conducting tissue below the bark
Potential diseases: Wilts
See the following:
Dutch elm disease (*p.71*)
Fusarium wilt (*p.43*)
Verticillium wilt (*p.43*)

Symptoms: Stems covered with slimy growth and die back
Potential disease: Slime flux
See the following:
Clematis slime flux (*p.84*)

Symptoms: Small brownish black shells attached to the stems, sometimes with sticky foliage
Potential pest: Scale insects
See the following:
Brown scale (*p.110*)
Euonymus scale (*p.80*)
Hemispherical and soft scales (*p.137*)
Horse chestnut scale (*p.72*)
Hydrangea scale (*p.80*)
Wisteria scale (*p.85*)

Roots, bulbs, and tubers
Symptoms: Root rot causing branches to die back

Potential diseases: Honey fungus (*p.43*), *Phytophthora* (*p.42*)
See the following:
Damping off (*p.139*)
Pansy sickness (*p.99*)
Roses (*p.86*)
Yew Phytophthora root rot (*p.77*)
Wisteria die-back (*p.85*)

Symptom: Large woody gall on roots
Potential disease: Crown gall (*p.68*)

Symptom: Roots thickened and distorted into a swollen mass
Potential disease: Clubroot (*p.109*)

Symptom: Small holes in tubers, onion bulbs, or other root vegetables
Potential pests: Slugs (*p.34*), wireworms (*p.108*)

Symptoms: Roots eaten and plants often wilt
Potential pest: Cutworms (*p.108*)
See the following:
Cabbage root fly (*p.115*)
Carrot fly (*p.121*)
Chafer grubs (*p.104*)
Leatherjackets (*p.104*)
Onion fly (*p.120*)
Vine weevil grubs (*pp.33 and 138*)

See also Bulbs, corms, tubers, and rhizomes (*pp.100–103*)

Apple and pear canker

Honey fungus

Crown gall

Controlling pests and diseases

Not everything in the garden is lovely and sooner or later pests and diseases will become apparent. Some can be tolerated, but others may require action to prevent them becoming a more severe problem. This can be achieved by various means, including the use of insecticides and fungicides, natural enemies, physical barriers, and other non-chemical treatments. Correct identification of the cause of the problem is essential so that appropriate measures can be taken at the right time.

ow chemicals work

ect chemicals depending on the
nt, pest, or disease that needs to be
ated. Sometimes a combination of
ethods might be required to eradicate

the problem. Use chemicals only if the
damage could be significant and cannot
be minimized using other techniques,
such as those listed on pages 56–63.

oosing the right chemical

use a chemical when it is recommended for the
ose you have in mind. It is illegal to use a pesticide
gicide or insecticide) on plants not listed on the
l. For example, a chemical such as myclobutanil,
conazole, or triticonazole labelled to control rusts on
mentals can also be used to control other diseases on
er ornamentals. Try the chemical on a few leaves first
ake sure there are no adverse effects on the plant.

use chemicals when necessary. Many pests
diseases can be kept at bay by good cultivation
niques, as described on pages 6–23. In addition,
uraging beneficial creatures (see pp.60–63) can
n effective alternative to using chemical sprays.

e organic pesticides, such as pyrethrum, fatty acids,
plant oils, are derived from plants, and others from
rally occurring chemicals, like sulphur. Once applied,
are quickly broken down into harmless products.

caterpillars off plants Picking caterpillars off
ly infested plants by hand is a more sensible way
ntrolling them than spraying. If the infestation is
re, then consider applying a contact insecticide,
as bifenthrin or pyrethrum.

Ladybirds These beetles are the best-known natural
predators of aphids. Lacewing larvae, hoverflies, tits, and
some midges also feed on aphids. Attract aphid eaters by
feeding birds or growing nettles. Cut down the nettles in
spring and the predators will spread through your garden.

Application methods

Chemicals vary in the way they work and it is important to know if you are using a contact or systemic pesticide. This influences how and when you apply the chemical.

Contact pesticides only kill insects or fungi that are hit by the spray or crawl over sprayed leaves. It is important to spray plants thoroughly, including both sides of the leaves.

Systemic pesticides are absorbed into the plant and are translocated to parts of the plant that have not been treated. They kill fungi within the plant tissues and are also useful in killing sap-feeding insects, which are difficult to reach with contact insecticides.

Preventive pesticides form a protective barrier on the surface of plants that stops fungi or bacteria penetrating. Apply them thoroughly to the plant before infection or infestation occurs. A few systemic fungicides also have some protective action.

Most pesticides available to gardeners have a broad spectrum of activity. This means that most pests, including beneficial insects, may be killed if the insecticide is applied, so use them strictly according to the manufacturer's instructions. Chemicals may be available as concentrated liquid sprays or drenches, ready-to-use sprays and pump guns, dusts, and pellets.

Liquids Liquid concentrate is cheap, but needs to be diluted to the volume required and needs special equipment for application. Ready-to-use sprays are already diluted at the appropriate concentrations, but they are only useful if small areas need to be treated.

Dusts Only a few contact chemicals are available as dusts. Although they leave an unsightly deposit, they are easy to apply on the targeted organism and little is wasted as dusts are used directly from the pack. For example, sulphur dusts kill powdery mildew spores as they germinate.

Pellets A few pests can be controlled by pellets, such as slugs and snails. They are poisoned baits in which the chemical has been mixed with something palatable. Follow the manufacturer's instructions and scatter slug pellets thinly as they can harm pets, children, and wildlife if eaten.

Using chemicals

Use garden chemicals with care to minimize any adverse effect they may have on the environment. Their safe storage and disposal is equally important, although this is quite often overlooked by the gardener. For full effectiveness and safety, follow the instructions on the label. Safety rules should also apply to the equipment you use to treat plants.

Mixing and applying chemicals

Follow the instructions on the manufacturer's label and apply the chemical at the stated rate and as described since this is often crucial to control the pest or disease. It is illegal to mix your own blends, including using washing-up liquid to kill aphids. Many chemicals are also incompatible. When a proprietary product contains both an insecticide and fungicide, use an alternative product if only a pest or disease has been a problem on the plant to be treated.

Measuring When making up solutions from concentrates, use water from a jug or similar container rather than diluting directly from a tap or hosepipe. Don't make up more than necessary to avoid having to dispose of the surplus.

Mixing Pour concentrated pesticide in the sprayer already partially filled with water. Rinse the measurer and use the rinsed out water to make up the solution. Make up to the final volume and close the container before mixing and applying the chemical.

Applying Spray the plants, including stems, buds, and both surfaces of leaves. Avoid excessive run-off. Apply at dusk or early morning on dry and still days to avoid scorching, harming beneficial insects, and to optimize chemical action.

Equipment If only small areas need to be treated, for example plants in a glasshouse, a ready-to-use spray might be the best option. A cheaper alternative is to use a small hand-pump sprayer, which you can keep refilling when necessary. When large areas need to be treated, you might need to buy special equipment, such as a sprayer with an external pump. Watering cans fitted with a dribble bar are particularly suitable for soil drenching. As for all pesticide applicators, they should be clearly labelled and used for no other purposes. Especially do not use the same container for weedkillers and pesticides as your plants could end up being severely damaged.

Storage Pesticide products are best stored at an even temperature. Concentrates will store for two years or more if kept in cool, dark conditions. Diluted concentrates can become ineffective after just 24 hours, so remember to only dilute enough for one day's use.

Safety For safety reasons, it is illegal to store pesticides that are unlabelled and not in their original container. Ready-to-use sprays can be more convenient for smaller areas, requiring no mixing and keeping just as long. Never dispose of surplus pesticide down drains, ditches, or in watercourses because of the risk of contaminating water and harming wildlife. Instead, dilute small quantities and spray onto permitted plants according to the manufacturer's instructions. Once rinsed thoroughly, place empty containers in household waste, rather than recycling them. Add the rinsing to the final spray solution or dispose of it as for surplus pesticides. When pesticides are withdrawn from the market, usually for economic reasons, there is a grace period of one to two years in which to use up stock. Contact your local authority's waste disposal section for disposal of larger quantities of pesticides. They can advise on which household sites take chemicals. Find details at www.pesticidedisposal.org.

Lock pesticides away Store them in a dark, cool place, out of reach of children, pets, and wildlife, preferably locked in a garden shed or garage, not in the house. Keep chemicals in their original containers, tightly closed and clearly labelled. Dispose of obsolete products safely.

Use gardening gloves Take care not to spill any chemicals and wear gloves when handling them. Wash your hands and face immediately if you accidentally splash chemicals on them. Take particular care if products bear a black cross with the words "harmful" or "irritant".

Use a designated watering can Thoroughly wash watering cans and sprayers after use. Even small residues of weedkillers can harm plants. Dispose of rinsed water safely, not into drains or near ponds and water courses. Do not mix different products.

Non-chemical controls: traps

Some traps can be used to reduce the numbers of certain pests, while other traps are used to monitor pest numbers and indicate the appropriate time to take additional control measures.

Setting traps

Trapping is a technique that can be used successfully in the garden against various invertebrate pests, such as slugs and snails, as well as some mammals. Setting traps for mammals, such as rats, mice, moles, grey squirrels, and rabbits, requires a bit of knowledge about the animals' behaviour patterns, since careful placement of traps in locations frequented by the animals will increase the chances of success. Some traps are designed to kill the animal outright, while others are cages that capture the animal alive for subsequent humane disposal, which is not a job for the squeamish. Trapping and disposing of invertebrate pests is an easier matter.

Sticky traps Yellow plastic sheets covered with a non-drying glue capture pests such as whitefly, thrips, and fungus gnats in greenhouses. These traps can be used to detect glasshouse whitefly before plants become too heavily infested for biological control to be effective.

Grease bands Apply grease bands to the trunks and stakes of fruit trees in the autumn. The wingless female of winter moths emerge from pupae in the soil and crawl up the trunk to lay eggs on the branches. Sticky bands ensure that some females fail to make the journey.

Slug traps Slugs and snails hide in dark damp places during the day. Placing pieces of cardboard, tiles, or similar materials on the soil provides them with hiding places from which they can be removed. Slugs can also be lured into beer-filled containers sunk into the soil, where they drown.

Wasp traps Wasps are attracted to sweet substances, especially in mid- to late summer. Make a trap by half filling a jam jar with water and jam. Cover the top with paper with a 1cm (½in) hole in the centre. Attracted by the fermenting contents, wasps will enter the jar and drown.

Pheromone traps Pheromones are produced by insects to attract a mate. For some pests, such as codling moth, use traps containing the attractant scent. Only males are caught but the traps record the flight period for more accurate timing of sprays against newly hatched caterpillars.

Mole traps Several mole traps are available, such as the Duffus trap shown here. Set and place the trap in the mole's tunnel and then cover to exclude light. Check the trap at least once a day. Reset it in another part of the tunnel system if the mole keeps pushing soil into the trap.

Rabbit traps Traps designed to kill rabbits can be set inside the mouth of burrows, or cage traps for live capture can be used. Entice rabbits into cage traps by scattering carrots inside and around the trap. Control captured rabbits by shooting or a sharp blow at the back of the head.

Non-chemical controls: barriers and repellents

Pest damage can sometimes be avoided or reduced by placing a physical barrier in the affected area that excludes the pest or presents a surface that the pest is reluctant to cross.

Where to use barriers

Barriers may not enhance the appearance of a garden, but they can be an effective means of keeping pests away from plants. Barriers, such as those described here, are more frequently used in vegetable plots than flower borders. They are particularly useful for protecting plants at vulnerable stages in their growth, such as seedlings, transplants, young shoots on herbaceous plants, and new plantings. Once plants have made some growth and become established, it is usually safe to remove the protective covers. It is undesirable to leave plants covered up for too long as the covers may reduce light, resulting in decidedly weak and spindly plants. They can also become overcrowded or run out of space.

Copper tape Slugs and snails have an aversion to copper and when confronted by a copper strip fixed around a pot or tub will usually turn away, rather than cross it. These pests can also be deterred by standing plant containers on mats impregnated with copper salts.

Tree guards Rabbits gnaw the bark from the trunks and stem bases on trees and shrubs, especially in the winter months. This can be fatal for the plant if most of the bark is lost. Protect woody plants by placing a collar or tree guard around the base of the trunk.

Rabbit deterrent Rabbits are attracted to new plantings. To keep them at bay, place covers over the plants or erect a barrier of wire netting around the plants. This enables new plants to get established and better able to survive rabbit grazing when the covers are removed.

Protect young plants Slugs and snails can quickly demolish seedlings and soft young shoots, which can be protected by placing cloches, made from plastic bottles from which the top and bottom has been removed, over the seedlings. Remove before they get too leggy.

Fine mesh netting Place finely woven horticultural fleeces over vegetables such as carrots and brassicas to exclude the egg-laying females of pests, such as carrot fly and cabbage root fly, for which there are no pesticides available for garden use. Keep in place until autumn.

Brassica collars Cabbage root fly lays its eggs in the soil close to the stems of its host plants. Place homemade or bought collars about 12cm (5in) across around the base of brassica transplants to prevent the flies placing eggs near by. Eggs laid on the collars dry up and fail to hatch.

Scarecrows While scarecrows can add to the fun of a garden, they are usually of little benefit in protecting plants from birds and other pests. Unless there is some real danger associated with a scaring device, birds, rabbits, and deer quickly become accustomed to it and ignore it.

Beneficial creatures

Not all insects and other garden wildlife are pests! Some are of real benefit to gardeners as pollinators of flowers or as predators or parasites of pests.

When is a pest not a pest?

Most of the fruits we grow need pollen to be transferred from one flower to another in order for the fruit to develop. Many vegetables and ornamental flowers also require pollination so they can set seed. Many insects can perform this task, but bees are particularly efficient as pollinators.

Animals become garden pests when they are sufficiently abundant to have an adverse effect on plants. In the absence of natural checks, such as predators, parasites, and diseases, pests rapidly increase in numbers. Fortunately, most gardens have an array of large and small animals that feed on pest species. These beneficial animals are not always effective in preventing pest infestations but without them, the situation could be a lot worse. The most effective predators or parasites are those that target specific pests.

Bumblebees

Bumblebees are social insects that live in nests, usually underground but also at ground level or in bird nest boxes. They are valuable in the garden as they will pollinate flowers during weather when honeybees stay in their hives. Each nest contains a queen bee and up to 200 worker bees. The nest is initiated in late spring by the queen and builds up to peak strength in late summer. Male bees and next year's queens are produced in late summer, after which the colony dies out. Only young queens overwinter.

Honeybees

Like bumblebees, honeybees are social insects headed by a queen bee, but with colonies of up to 60,000 workers. These semi-domesticated insects are kept by beekeepers in hives. Honeybees differ from bumblebees by surviving the winter as an active colony, so large numbers of worker bees are available for pollination duty in spring when fruit trees blossom. In addition to their role as pollinators, honeybees provide us with other products, such as honey and beeswax.

Lacewings

Some lacewings have green bodies that are 8–22mm (³/₈–³/₄in) long, but other species are black or brown. The adult insects feed on pollen and nectar, while their larvae are voracious predators of aphids and other small insects. Lacewings have long, thread-like antennae and are named after their attractive, multi-veined wings. The larvae have elongate bodies and a pair of sharp curved jaws with which they seize their prey. Some lacewing larvae disguise themselves by covering their backs with a layer of sucked-out aphid skins.

Hoverfly larvae

The legless hoverfly maggots have flattened bodies up to 12mm (¹/₂in) long, and are often found on aphid-infested plants during the summer. A single larva can devour up to 600 aphids before it is fully fed and ready to pupate. The colours of adult hoverflies are often mainly black with yellow bands or other markings on their abdomens. Their name comes from their ability to hover in flight. Like lacewings, adult hoverflies feed on nectar and pollen.

Flower bugs

These predatory insects, also known as anthocorid bugs, are 3–5mm (¹/₈–¹/₄in) long. The adult flower bugs and their nymphs insert needle-like mouthparts into the eggs or bodies of small insects and mites in order to suck out the contents. They are active from spring to autumn, spending the winter hidden in sheltered places. Some flower bug species live mainly on trees and can be useful predators of pests on fruit trees, such as aphids, suckers, and red spider mites.

Beneficial creatures *continued*

Frogs and toads

These amphibians eat a wide range of insects, slugs, woodlice, and other small creatures. They do most of their feeding at night during spring to autumn. A garden pond provides somewhere for frogs and toads to breed in the spring.

Ladybirds

Both the adult beetles and larvae of most ladybirds are predatory insects. Many ladybirds prey on aphids, but others specialize in feeding on scale insects, mealybugs, or red spider mites. The adults are often red or yellow with varying numbers of black spots; others are brown or orange and have white spots. The larvae, however, have less distinctive markings. They are black with orange or white markings and are up to 12mm (½in) long. Ladybird larvae can eat up to 500 aphids, and probably as many again when they become adult insects.

Shrews

Shrews are small mammals that are largely nocturnal and so not often seen. They eat large numbers of insects, spiders, worms, and slugs. Shrews have characteristic pointed snouts that separate them from similar-sized mice and voles.

Centipedes

These insects have elongate segmented bodies that are orange brown or pale yellow. Each body segment bears a single pair of legs, unlike millipedes that have two pairs per segment. The front pair of legs curves forward and is modified to act as jaws. Some centipedes live and hunt for small creatures on the soil surface. They are up to 30mm (1¼in) long. Other centipedes, however, live in the soil and these often have much longer and more slender bodies.

Song thrush

Song thrushes feed on worms, insects, and berries, but they also eat large numbers of snails from the garden, especially during the period when they are rearing their young. The bird holds a snail in its beak and smashes the shell against a stone to break it open. This habit, together with their melodic song, makes song thrushes welcome garden residents. They nest in trees and shrubs and can raise two broods of three to five chicks during the summer months.

Biological controls

Biological control is the use of a natural enemy to control a pest. Some parasites, predators, and pathogenic nematodes can be purchased for this purpose.

Predators, such as ladybirds and larvae of hoverflies and lacewings, capture their prey and kill it quickly.

Parasitic wasps and flies lay eggs on or inside the eggs or bodies of a suitable host insect or other invertebrate animal. They hatch into larvae that initially cause no obvious harm to the host insect, which continues feeding and growing. Eventually the parasite larvae destroy the host insect's vital organs and, at that point, the host insect is killed and the parasite larvae emerge and pupate.

Pathogenic nematodes are microscopic worm-like animals that invade the bodies of various pests, mainly those that live in the soil. These nematodes release bacteria that infect the host animal with a fatal disease. Such nematodes are used against vine weevil grubs, chafer grubs, leatherjackets and slugs.

Aphid parasite laying an egg in an aphid
Parasitic wasps, such as *Aphidius* and *Praon* species, lay single eggs inside the bodies of young aphids. The aphids continue feeding and growing but are unable to reproduce. The parasite larva developing inside the aphid eventually kills it. Parasitized aphids become brown or black and abnormally inflated and rounded shortly before they die. The parasite pupates inside or under the dead aphid's body.

Pathogenic nematodes
These microscopic eelworms or nematodes are watered into the soil or potting compost to control pests, such as slugs and vine weevil grubs, or lawn pests, such as chafer grubs and leatherjackets. Different species of nematode are required for these pests. The nematodes, which give the pests a fatal bacterial infection, need to be applied to moist soil at a time when soil temperatures are sufficiently high to allow the nematodes to be active during spring to early autumn.

Predatory aphid midge
The larvae of a tiny fly, *Aphidoletes aphidimyza*, prey on greenfly and other aphids. The orange larvae, which are up to 3mm (⅛in) long, insert their mouthparts into the leg joints of aphids and then suck out the body contents. Each midge larva will control about 60 aphids before it then goes into the soil to pupate. This biological control can be purchased for use in greenhouses, but the fly also occurs in gardens on aphid-infested plants throughout the summer.

Trees, shrubs, and climbers

Trees can be difficult to treat if they are affected by a pest or disease, quite simply because of their size. However, many problems on young trees may be prevented – or stabilized – by maintaining good hygiene and tackling any problems as soon as they become apparent. The same goes for shrubs and climbers, especially by ensuring that, where necessary, you prune your plants regularly and at the right time to prevent congestion.

Trees, shrubs, and climbers: general pests and diseases

The pests and diseases described on these pages and overleaf can affect many of the plants found in this section. Host-specific pests and diseases are described in their relevant groups.

The plant divisions in this chapter are:
- Trees (*see pp.70–75*)
- Conifers and hedges (*see pp.76–77*)
- Shrubs (*see pp.78–81*)
- Azaleas, camellias, and rhododendrons (*see pp.82–83*)
- Climbers (*see pp.84–85*)
- Roses (*see pp.86–87*)

Gall mites These microscopic mites induce various abnormal growths or galls on the foliage and buds. Their feeding causes abnormally enlarged buds (big buds), or on leaves, the excessive growth of hairs (felt galls), raised pimples, or cylindrical structures (nail galls), or thickening and curling of leaf margins.

Cushion scale This sap-sucking pest is found on camellia, holly, rhododendron, *Trachelospermum*, and other evergreen shrubs. Coatings of sooty mould develop

Although galls on foliage and buds may look worrying, gall mites have little impact on plant growth. There is no effective treatment.

Control newly hatched scale nymphs by spraying them with thiacloprid or acetamiprid in early summer.

Caterpillars can sometimes be removed by hand, but for heavy infestations, use bifenthrin or pyrethrum.

on the insect's excrement on the upper leaf surface. The mature insects are 3–4mm (⅛in) long and lay eggs in elongate white waxy bands on the underside of leaves.

Moths Caterpillars of moths, such as buff tip (*see opposite, bottom right*), brown-tail, lackey, and yellow-tail, eat the foliage of many trees and shrubs. Some, such as leopard moth caterpillars, tunnel in trunks and branches.

Adelgids These small, sap-sucking insects are closely related to aphids. They only attack conifers, especially spruce, pine, larch, and douglas fir. The insects are covered in fluffy white wax or concealed inside galls. Small conifers can be sprayed with bifenthrin, thiacloprid, or acetamiprid when adelgids become active in early spring, but they have to be tolerated on large trees.

Coral spot This disease is caused by the fungus *Nectria cinnabarina* and is commonly seen on dead twigs of trees and shrubs, or woody debris such as pea sticks. It causes problems on plants that are suffering from other stresses. In damp weather, small pink or red cushion-like eruptions are evident on affected bark. The fungus can infect through wounds and, once established, kills branches rapidly. *Magnolia*, *Eleagnus*, *Acer*, figs, currants, and gooseberries are frequently affected.

Adelgids cause little real damage to mature trees, but for smaller ones, see above for treatment suggestions.

To limit entry points for coral spot infection, carefully prune dead wood. If the problem persists, a wound sealant can help.

Trees, shrubs and climbers: general pest and diseases: *continued*

Witches' broom These are abnormal twig proliferations that are mostly caused by a fungus that can lead to a reduction in flowering. Many trees can be affected including species of *Abies*, *Betula*, *Prunus*, and *Salix*.

Canker These are dead sections of bark on branches or main trunks of trees. Canker diseases may cause extensive damage to trees when they kill all of the bark in a particular area, thus girdling a branch or main stem. If the trunk is affected, the entire plant may die. Examples of canker diseases are coryneum and phomopsis cankers (confined to *Cupressaceae*), and nectria canker, which mostly damages pears and apples, but can affect other broadleaved trees such as rowan, beech, ash, and holly.

Crown gall This bacterial gall affects many plants, but particularly fruit trees and cane fruits. Plants may struggle and upon examination a large woody gall is found at ground level or on the roots caused by soil-borne bacteria parasitise that injure roots or the stem and cause the tissue to proliferate. Avoid planting diseased specimens or injuring roots.

Witches' brooms are only likely to impair flowering potential, but can be cut out of the tree if necessary.

For most cankers, cutting out affected branches below the infected bark retards development. Apply a wound paint to avoid reinfection.

If crown gall is present, grow some potatoes in place of the existing crop and avoid replanting with a susceptible species.

Removing the fruiting body of wood decay fungus does not stop the disease; they usually only appear when infection is well established.

Wood decay fungi Many different fungi can cause wood decay. Some cause top rots, where airborne spores enter wounds in the canopy and cause branch decay. Others cause root and butt rots, and may be indicated by crown thinning and early leaf loss. Often the first indication of decay will be the appearance of fungal fruiting bodies. Commonly these are brackets, but toadstools and elaborate structures or encrustations are also possible. It is wise to seek professional advice regarding the safety of the tree.

Tree scabs Several trees are affected by scabs caused by fungi. The most significant foliar scab disease is apple and pear scab, which also attacks *Cotoneaster*, rowans, hawthorns, and, less commonly, *Pyracantha*. In addition, there are other fungal species causing scabs on *Pyracantha*, olive, loquat, and willow. Symptoms of tree scabs include dark green patches, which can be seen on the leaves and eventually lead to dead tissues. Dark sunken spots also appear on fruits or berries. Infected leaves then fall prematurely. Recurring infection causes poor growth and die-back of defoliated trees. The disease can be controlled on apples and pears by spraying chemicals such as myclobutanil. The latter can also be used if trees are grown as ornamentals. Varieties resistent to tree scabs are available.

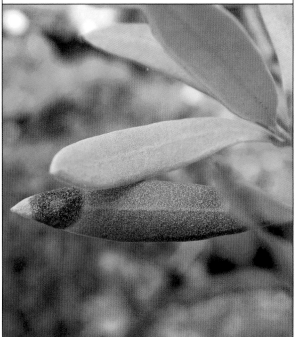

If a plant has tree scabs, destroy fallen leaves or spray with a fungicide such as myclobutanil.

Trees

Several pests and diseases that affect trees are well known to us because of the significance these large plants play in our landscape and heritage.

If you have damage on:
- Acer, see also hydrangea scale (*p.80*) and wisteria scale (*p.85*)
- Hawthorn and *Sorbus*, see pear and cherry slugworm (*p.123*)
- Lime or sycamore, see also horse chestnut scale (*p.72*)

See also:
- General pests and diseases on trees, shrubs, and climbers (*pp.66–69*)
- Know your enemy: pests and diseases (*pp.26–43*)
- Winter moth (*p.110*)

Arbutus leaf spots
Arbutus can be affected by several leaf spot fungi (*see p.40*), including *Septoria unedonis* and *Elsinoë mattirolianum*. The damage by the latter can be severe. The only recommended course of action is to remove the fallen material to reduce infection for the following year. Also, cut back dying branches to healthy tissue.

Beech woolly aphid
The foliage on beech trees and hedges is infested during late spring and summer by dense colonies of pale yellow aphids covered in fluffy white waxy secretions. The leaves become sticky with excreted honeydew. Only hedges and small trees can be treated. Spray when aphids are first seen with pyrethrum, bifenthrin, thiacloprid, or acetamiprid.

Acer pimple gall
The foliage of sycamore, field maple, and Japanese acers is affected by this tiny mite. It sucks sap from the lower leaf surface and causes hollow reddish bumps or pimples to grow on the top side of the leaves. During the summer, the mites live and feed inside the pimple galls. No serious damage is caused, so control measures are not required.

Tar spot of Acer
It is the fungus *Rhytisma acerinum* that causes tar spot of Acer. The symptoms are large black blotches on the leaves, which are slightly raised and shiny. All the infections in a season arise from spores that have been produced from the previous year's infected over-wintered leaves. Tar spot of Acer is mainly observed on sycamores, although other maples may be affected. Fortunately, this disease is not very damaging to the tree since its vigour is not often affected. Although there is no chemical control for this particular disease, removing and burning the fallen infected material (*see p.18*), which can occur prematurely, will help to reduce the infection in the following year.

Eucalyptus sucker

Shoot tips and young leaves are infested with the grey or orange flattened nymphs of this sap-sucking insect. Heavily infested shoots may have the tips killed. A greyish green sooty mould can develop on the insect's sticky excrement. On trees small enough to be sprayed, treat with thiacloprid or acetamiprid when signs of infestation are seen.

Eucalyptus gall wasp

This tiny black insect lays eggs in eucalyptus leaves in early summer. Small pinkish pustules develop, each containing a single grub. The galls later become greyish brown. Heavily infested leaves may drop prematurely. On trees small enough to be sprayed, treat with thiacloprid or acetamiprid in early summer. Dispose of fallen leaves before adult gall wasps emerge.

Dutch elm disease

The first signs are browning and yellowing of the leaves. The affected branches die back from the tips and discoloured leaves then fall. Symptoms spread until the tree dies. The disease is caused by two fungi and is disseminated by elm bark beetles. Destroy infected trees. There are varieties that are claimed to have good resistance.

Dogwood anthracnose

The symptoms of this fungus are brown spots on the leaves, perhaps with purplish margins surrounded by a yellowish halo. The spot may spread to form a more extensive blotch. Leaves shrivel and small stems may be killed. Defoliation usually starts earlier. Prune out and dispose of infected material. The disease can be devastating, but trees may recover.

Elm gall mite

In late spring, elms develop hard raised swellings on the upper surface of their leaves. These are induced by microscopic gall mites that live and feed within these galls. The mites overwinter underneath the bud scales. No serious damage is caused to the tree, apart from creating the galls. This is fortunate as there are no effective controls.

Trees *continued*

Horse chestnut bleeding canker

Bleeding patches develop on the bark and trees decline. Traditionally this was ascribed to *Phytophthora* (see p.42), but the recent epidemic appears to be caused by a bacterium. Do not cut out infected limbs as this creates new entry points. Unless affected trees are a health hazard, they are best left alone and may recover if they have vigorous crowns.

Horse chestnut leaf blotch

This leaf blotch disease is caused by the fungus *Guignardia aesculi*. As a result of the fungal infection, the leaves develop irregular blotches, which are often outlined by a yellow band, from midsummer onwards. The leaves may shrivel and fall prematurely. As the damage occurs late in the season, the health of the tree is usually not affected.

Horse chestnut leaf-mining moth

Tiny caterpillars feed within the leaves, causing elongate white or brown blotch mines. There are at least three generations and by late summer most of the foliage may have turned brown. Control is generally not possible because of the size of the tree. The damage is disfiguring, but the tree won't be killed. *Aesculus indica* is resistant to this pest.

Horse chestnut scale

This sap-sucking insect is most easily seen in early summer when females deposit their eggs on the bark of horse chestnut, lime, sycamore, and other acers. The eggs are laid under a white waxy substance on which the scale's brown shell is perched. Use thiacloprid or acetamiprid in midsummer on small trees and shrubs to control the newly hatched nymphs.

Lime nail gall mite

During the summer, upright cylindrical structures 3–5mm (1/8–1/4in) tall and yellowish green or red in colour grow on the upper leaf surface of lime trees. The hollow galls contain microscopic mites whose feeding activities have induced the galls' growth. No real damage is done and as there is no effective treatment, this gall mite has to be tolerated.

Holm oak leaf miner

Two species of leaf-mining moths cause problems on holm oak. The more widespread species causes elongate blotch mines where the caterpillars have eaten out the internal tissues. The other species, which is found in the London area, creates wiggly linear mines. Neither moth can be controlled effectively, so damage has to be tolerated.

Oak processionary moth

The gregarious caterpillars of the oak processionary moth are covered with greyish hairs that cause an irritating rash if they come into contact with skin. An infestation by oak processionary caterpillars can result in severe defoliation, especially when young trees are affected. The larvae feed on oak and some other deciduous trees in late spring to early summer. This new pest in Britain is currently confined to southeast England, where attempts are being made to eradicate it. Report suspected infestations of the oak processionary moth to the Forestry Commission (www.forestry.gov.uk), which will advise you on the required control measures that have been put in place for this pest.

Oak gall wasps

More than 30 species of gall wasps occur on common oak. Their larvae cause various abnormal growths, known as galls, on the foliage, buds, catkins, acorns, roots, and stems. Spangle galls and silk button galls (see above) occur on the leaves in late summer. None of these gall wasps causes any real damage, so control measures are not required.

Acorn gall wasp

The female gall wasp lays eggs in early summer when oak acorns begin to form. The grubs develop inside the acorns and cause the formation of a ridged woody gall, which entirely or partly replaces the acorn. The gall is fully developed by late summer. Apart from destroying some of an oak tree's seeds, this gall wasp causes no harm. There are no control measures.

Oak powdery mildew

Powdery mildew species that affect oak can be seen as a white, thin, powdery-like coating sometimes associated with dead patches on the leaves. Premature defoliation occurs, but the vigour of mature trees is rarely affected. Fungicide treatments for oak powdery mildew are not necessary unless the trees are young.

Trees *continued*

Mountain ash gall mite

In late spring, the leaves of rowan or mountain ash develop whitish green blotches where microscopic mites are feeding inside the leaves. The discoloured areas darken until by midsummer the leaves have many brown blotches. There is no effective treatment. In years when trees are heavily infested, they can look very unhealthy but will survive.

Walnut gall mite

In summer, walnut leaves develop raised "blisters" on the upper leaf surface. The underside of these blisters is covered in creamy white hairs among which live the microscopic mites. Apart from creating the galls, the mites have no harmful effect on the tree's growth or ability to produce nuts. There are no effective pesticide treatments.

Plane anthracnose

This fungal disease is specific to London plane. The spores require wet conditions in which to germinate, and are also splashed around in rain droplets. Symptoms vary and include premature leaf fall, twig dieback, and browning on either side of the main leaf vein. Vigour of trees is not usually affected. No fungicide treatment is available, nor is it necessary.

Quince leaf blight

Irregular brown spots develop on the leaves of quince and other plants in the *Rosaceae* family, which blacken and fall prematurely. Shoots or fruits can be attacked. Infections proliferate in the summer and the fungus overwinters on shoots. Infected tissues and fallen leaves should be disposed of. The variety 'Krymsk' is supposedly resistant to the disease.

Robinia decline

Since 2007, *Robinia* 'Frisia' has been declining. Branches die back and the tree ultimately dies. Several factors thought to contribute to this include unusually wet summers, a leaf-spot fungus, and root diseases such as honey fungus and *Phytophthora* (see pp.42–43), and Phomopsis die-back. Prune affected trees to help limit the spread of *Phomopsis*.

Poplar canker
The bacterium *Xanthomonas populi* infects through wounds and natural openings. It overwinters in bark cankers and, in spring, bacterium ooze out of bark cracks and spread by wind or rain splash. It causes die-back on young branches. On large branches and stems, large cankers may develop. As symptoms appear, cut out infected parts.

Willow leaf beetle
The foliage of willows and poplars develop brown, dried-up patches where the 3–4mm (⅛in) long, metallic bronzy green adult beetles and their black larvae have grazed away the leaf surface. By late summer, the foliage may have been extensively damaged. On small trees, spray with bifenthrin, thiacloprid, or acetamiprid when damage is seen.

Willow bark aphid
Dense colonies of a large greyish black aphid occur on the bark of willow branches and trunks in late summer. They excrete a sticky honeydew that often attracts wasps. Little real damage is done to the tree, but the stickiness and wasps can be a nuisance. If necessary, small willows can be sprayed with pyrethrum, bifenthrin, thiacloprid, or acetamiprid.

Willow bean gall sawfly
Hard red or yellowish-green bean-shaped swellings, about 6mm (¼in) long, develop in willow leaves in early and late summer. Each gall contains a caterpillar-like larva that gradually hollows out the gall. Damage is confined to the creation of the galls and the tree's health and vigour is unimpaired. Control measures are therefore not required.

Willow black canker
Black canker is caused by a fungus that infects older twigs and smaller branches, and overwinters in lesions on the stems. Infections first cause irregular black spots on the leaves, which spread to the stems. The disease is prevalent in cool, wet weather when new foliage appears. Some varieties are more resistant. This disease must be tolerated.

Willow anthracnose
Small brown spots caused by a fungus appear on leaves, leading to early defoliation, and black cankers form on stems, causing die-back. In damp seasons, willow anthracnose can be extremely damaging. Trees will recover in drier years, however, and the disease must be tolerated. *Salix x sepulcralis* var. *chrysocoma* is the worst affected.

Conifers and hedges

A sick hedge or conifer can be a constant source of irritation for a gardener if the desired effect is for a uniform colour or shape.

If you have damage on:
- Juniper, see pear rust (*p.123*)
- Privet, see lilac leaf miner (*p.78*) in addition to privet thrips (*below*)
- Silver fir, see fuchsia rust (*p.79*)

See also:
- General pests and diseases on trees, shrubs, and climbers (*pp.66–69*)
- Know your enemy: pests and diseases (*pp.26–43*)

Green spruce aphid
This small, dark green aphid is active from autumn to spring on *Picea* species, especially Norway spruce. The foliage becomes mottled and drops in late winter or spring. New growth is in sharp contrast to the damaged foliage. Spray with pyrethrum, bifenthrin, thiacloprid, or acetamiprid if aphids or damage are seen. Damaged trees will take several years to recover.

Conifer red spider mite
Tiny, yellowish green mites suck sap from the foliage of conifers, especially spruce. This causes a fine mottling of the foliage, which gradually becomes yellowish brown as the summer progresses. It is mainly a problem on small conifers in sunny positions. If necessary, spray with bifenthrin when damage is detected. A hand lens will aid detection of the mite.

Cypress aphid
This aphid is a common cause of extensive die-back on *Cupressus*, *Chamaecyparis* and Leyland cypress hedges in late summer. Lower parts are worst affected. Black sooty moulds, which grow on aphid excrement, may be seen on infested stems. Spray with thiacloprid or acetamiprid in late spring to prevent a damaging infestation developing.

Privet thrips
The foliage on privet hedges and lilac becomes silvery brown in late summer as a result of thrips sucking sap from the leaves. The adult thrips have narrow elongate bodies, 2mm (¹⁄₁₂ in) long, and are blackish brown with white bands across the wings. The nymphs are yellowish white. If necessary, spray with pyrethrum, bifenthrin, acetamiprid, or thiacloprid.

Holly leaf miner
Most hollies, especially clipped hedges, have some leaf miner damage, developing between early summer and spring. The maggots of a tiny fly feed inside the leaves, causing yellowish-purple blotch mines. Although unsightly, the damage is small. Due to the thick waxy surface of holly leaves, sprays are ineffective against the leaf miner.

Holly leaf blight

Symptoms are circular black spots on the leaves, which fall rapidly. *Phytophthora itius* also infects young stems, leading to black lesions. In hedges, infections spread to form "arches" of defoliation. There are no fungicides available to amateur gardeners, so control depends on hygiene, by ensuring that no infected plants are brought into the garden.

Escallonia leaf spots

There are two new leaf spots that are very damaging on escallonia. They cause brown/purple spots on the leaves and then defoliation and stem die-back. Remove fallen material and cut back infected branches to reduce disease spread. Myclobutanil, penconazole, and triticonazole labelled for other diseases on ornamentals may have some control.

Keithia thujina needle blight

The leaf blight fungus *Didymascella thujina* (syn. *Keithia thujina*) is specific to *Thuja*, usually a problem seen more in nurseries as it affects and can kill plants that are less than four years old. Susceptibility lessens with age. The fungus can be seen as black bodies on the dead leaves, later falling out to leave cavities. No control is necessary on outplanted trees.

Yew Phytophthora root rot

Yew is extremely susceptible to the root rot pathogen *Phytophthora*. Affected plants show bronze foliage and infection of fine roots causes the roots to snap, resulting in black discolouration of the root tips and a reduced root system. Remove affected plants, improve drainage and keep the area free of woody plants for at least three years.

Laurel diseases

Leaves of laurel are often affected by powdery mildew, leaf spot fungi, and bacterial shothole, all of which can cause holes, tattering, and distortion in the leaves. Application of a general fertilizer and foliar feed helps to boost the vigour of the tree. Fungicides such as myclobutanil, penconazole, or triticonazole may be used to control fungal problems.

Pestalotiopsis

In the last decade, *Pestalotiopsis* has been increasingly reported to cause widespread damage to a number of plants, including many conifers. The symptoms are browning, followed by death of the foliage. The only option is the removal of the dead and dying foliage. Minimize further infection by ensuring any healthy plants are kept in good condition.

Shrubs

The smaller size of shrubs means that problems are more apparent, being at eye level. It also means treatment of the whole plant is more feasible.

If you have damage on:
- Buddleia, see figwort weevil (*p.79*) and mullein moth (*p.92*)
- *Chaenomeles* and *Sorbus*, see pear and cherry slugworm (*p.123*)
- *Mahonia*, see mahonia rust (*p.81*) and berberis sawfly (*right*)
- *Phygelius*, see figwort weevil (*p.79*)

See also:
- General pests and diseases on trees, shrubs, and climbers (*pp.66–69*)

Berberis sawfly
Whitish green caterpillar-like larvae with black spots and yellow blotches defoliate some deciduous *Berberis*, especially *B. thunbergii*, and *Mahonia*. There are two or three generations between late spring and early autumn. When fully fed, the larvae go into the soil to pupate. Spray the young larvae with pyrethrum, bifenthrin, acetamiprid, or thiacloprid.

Broom gall mite
Whitish green cauliflower-like enlarged buds develop on the stems of broom (*Cytisus*) during the summer. These galls contain microscopic mites whose feeding has induced the abnormal growth. Later the galls become greyish brown and dry up. There is no effective chemical treatment. Pick off the galled buds or destroy heavily infested plants.

Gleditsia gall midge
From late spring onwards, gleditsia leaves fail to develop normally. The leaflets form small pods that contain several whitish orange maggots. Several generations occur over the summer months, with the degree of galling progressively building up. The leaf galls dry up and drop off, creating bare branch tips in late summer. There is no effective control.

Laburnum leaf miner
Laburnum foliage is mined by fly and moth larvae. Caterpillars of the latter create roughly circular whitish brown mines up to 10mm (½in) in diameter. Maggots of the leaf-mining fly make irregular blotch mines along the leaf margins. Neither cause serious harm as heavy infestations do not usually occur before late summer. There is no effective control.

Lilac leaf miner
Lilac and privet foliage develops large brown blotch mines in early and late summer where the caterpillars have eaten the internal tissues. When half grown, the caterpillars emerge and complete their feeding inside the rolled leaf tip, which is held in place with silk threads. Remove affected leaves on lilac or clip infested privet hedges to reduce the infestation.

Cotoneaster webber moth

Two moths with small dark brown caterpillars attack *Cotoneaster horizontalis*. Hawthorn webber moth caterpillars cover their feeding area with sheets of white silk. Porphyry knothorn caterpillars live in silk tubes spun along the stems. Both cause brown foliage, mainly in early summer. Spray caterpillars with bifenthrin or prune out infested shoots.

Pyracantha leaf miner

The foliage develops distinctive oval-shaped silvery white mines in the centre of the upper leaf surface where the caterpillar is feeding inside the leaf. The heaviest infestations are often in mid–late winter, but mined leaves can be found at other times of year. Little real damage is done, even when plants are heavily infested, so control measures are not required.

Figwort weevil

Several species of figwort weevils occur on figwort, buddleia, mullein, and *Phygelius*. The adults are 2–4mm ($\frac{1}{12}$–$\frac{1}{8}$in) long and greyish white with a circular black spot on the wing cases. The larvae are slimy, yellowish brown grubs which, like the adults, eat the foliage and flower buds. Spray the pests with bifenthrin, thiacloprid, or acetamiprid at dusk.

Elephant hawk moth on fuchsia

Fully grown caterpillars are about 80mm (3in) long and have two pairs of eye-like marking at the head end. Mature caterpillars are mainly blackish brown, but are sometimes green. They eat the foliage of many plants, but in gardens they feed mainly on fuchsia. Infestations usually consist of one or two caterpillars, so hand removal is feasible.

Fuchsia rust

It is the fungus *Pucciniastrum epilobii* that causes fuchsia rust. It also infects willow herbs (*Epilobium*) and alternates between them and silver firs (*Abies*). Yellow spots appear on the upper leaf surfaces corresponding to orange pustules on the lower surfaces, leading to death of leaves. Black overwintering spores have only been found on willow herbs. The fungal spores on willow herbs germinate in the spring and subsequently infect species of silver fir. Likewise, spores produced on firs can then infect fuchsias, although the disease may be present on fuchsia the whole year round. Fuchsias are sensitive to spray damage, so check the label of fungicides labelled for rust carefully before applying.

Shrubs *continued*

Pieris lacebug

A coarse, pale mottling develops on the upper leaf surface of pieris and rhododendron leaves. Adult pieris lacebugs are 3mm (⅛in) long and have transparent wings with black markings. Both adults and the spiny blackish brown nymphs live on the underside of the leaves from late spring to autumn. Spray them with thiacloprid or acetamiprid.

Hydrangea scale

The stems and undersides of leaves of hydrangea, *Acer*, and *Prunus* are covered with white, waxy, oval-shaped egg masses about 4mm (⅛in) long in early summer. This pest sucks sap from the foliage in the summer, and heavy infestations weaken plants. Control the scale by spraying the nymphs with thiacloprid or acetamiprid in midsummer.

Euonymus scale

Mainly found on the leaves and stems of *Euonymus japonicus*, where these insects suck sap. The tiny male scales have elongate white shells; females have blackish brown, pear-shaped coverings. Infested foliage develops a yellowish mottling, followed by leaf drop. Spray with thiacloprid or acetamiprid in midsummer and early autumn to control the young nymphs.

Box sucker

Damage is caused in late spring by the pale green, flattened immature nymphs of this sap-sucking insect. They stunt the new shoots and distort the leaves, giving shoot tips a cabbage-like appearance. This pest is not a problem for box that is clipped to restrict growth. Spray young plants with thiacloprid or acetamiprid when new shoots emerge.

Box blight

There are two fungi that can cause box leaves to go brown, followed by defoliation and die-back. *Cylindrocladium buxicola* causes black streaks on stems. *Volutella buxi* needs wounds or stressed plants to infect, but once it has taken hold in the main stem, the plant may die. *C. buxicola* is very damaging and difficult to control once present, so keep new plants separate from existing ones for a month to ensure they are clean. All box species are susceptible, but tightly clipped dwarf varieties are worst affected. To prevent box blight spreading further, destroy affected plants and fallen leaves and replace the top soil. Fungicides for use on ornamentals have limited success for both diseases.

Viburnum beetle

Only *Viburnum tinus* and *V. opulus*, are extensively defoliated by creamy white, black-marked beetle larvae, up to 9mm (⅜in) long, in mid- to late spring. Some further damage is caused by the greyish brown adult beetles in late summer. Look for holes in the new growth in April and then spray with bifenthrin, thiacloprid, or acetamiprid.

Viburnum whitefly

Viburnum tinus is attacked by this sap-sucking insect. The white-winged adults occur in summer and are 2mm (¹⁄₁₂in) long. It is the overwintering, black oval nymphs encrusted with white wax on the underside of leaves that are most often seen. Control is not usually required, but if necessary spray in midsummer with thiacloprid or acetamiprid.

Hebe downy mildew

Peronospora grisea can be seen underneath the leaves as a greyish fungus corresponding to yellow patches on the upper surfaces. The plants may subsequently be defoliated and growth of plants checked. No chemical control is available for hebe downy mildew so all you can do is destroy infected leaves or plants.

Mahonia rust

The symptoms of mahonia rust are orange or red purple spots on the top of leaves corresponding with dark brown spots on the underside. Heavy infections cause premature leaf drop. The disease enjoys humid air, so prune out the affected branches to improve ventilation and destroy fallen leaves. If necessary, spray with an approved fungicide for rusts.

Yucca leaf spot

The symptoms for this leaf spot are yellowish and brown lesions. They are generally elliptical and scattered across the upper surface of the leaves. There are no fungicides to control fungal leaf spots, but you can try myclobutanil, penconazole, and triticonazole. Remove the infected leaves and avoid overhead watering or protect from rainfall.

Azaleas, camellias, and rhododendrons

Fortunately, camellias and rhododendrons are not often affected by pests and diseases, and those that do arise are mostly treatable.

See also:
- General pests and diseases on trees, shrubs, and climbers (*pp.66–69*)
- Know your enemy: pests and diseases (*pp.26–43*)
- Pieris lacebug (*p.80*), powdery mildew (*p.40*), and *Phytophthora* (p.42), which can also affect rhododendrons

Azalea and camellia galls
Azalea gall causes dramatic swellings on the leaves of plants. The green galls become covered in a white spore bloom, which will spread the infection. Remove the galls by hand before they become white. A similar fungus causes large round or forked galls on camellias that also develop a white bloom. Plant vigour is not affected. Prune out promptly.

Camellia petal blight
Caused by *Ciborinia camelliae*, camellia petal blight begins with small brown flecks on the petals that eventually spread on the whole flowers. The flowers then fall early. It can be confused with frost damage, but if affected by the disease, a white or grey fungus can be seen under the petals when they are separated from the calyx. Dispose of affected flowers as there are no chemicals available. If you don't, the fungus forms a black structure at the base of the petals, which remains dormant until the next flowering season when it germinates to produce a fruiting body. This will release spores that are wind dispersed to land on petals and so the cycle continues. A deep mulch might also help to breakdown the cycle.

Camellia yellow mottle virus
Camellia yellow mottle virus causes bright yellow or creamy-white blotches or speckling on the dark green leaves. The virus may also cause flower breaking. The vigour of the plant is not affected, but prune out affected branches and do not propagate to help prevent the virus spreading. The vector for camellia yellow mottle is unknown.

Rhododendron leafhopper

Adult leafhoppers, which are 8mm (⅜in) long and turquoise green with red stripes, occur in late summer. The females lay overwintering eggs in next year's flower buds, creating infection sites for bud blast disease (*see below*). Remove dead buds as they develop and spray the plant in late summer with thiacloprid or acetamiprid to reduce egg laying.

Rhododendron leaf spots

The fungus *Glomerella cingulata* causes irregular purple brown spots. If only a few leaves are diseased, dispose of them together with any leaves showing brown patches. A systemic fungicide applied for powdery mildew may control this disease. Encourage vigour in affected shrubs by good cultivation, including the use of a foliar feed.

Rhododendron leaf blight

Several *Phytophthora* species, including *P. ramorum*, can cause leaf blight and twig die-back. Brown, spreading lesions develop on leaves, sometimes with a V-shaped appearance, followed by wilting and die back. Cut back infected shoots to healthy tissues. If you suspect *P. ramorum*, do not try to control it and report it to the Food and Environmental Research Agency.

Rhododendron rust

The upper leaf surfaces develop yellowish patches and, in the summer, fungal pustules containing orange and brown spores develop on the undersides. The fungus lives within affected leaves so they are infected until they fall. The disease, therefore, appears every season. Dispose of affected leaves and spray with an approved fungicide for rusts.

Rhododendron bud blast

Bud blast kills flower buds on rhododendrons leading to a reduction in flowers. The buds become covered in black, pinhead-like structures. This fungus (*Pycnostysanus azaleae*) is spread by the rhododendron leafhopper (*see above*), and control of the insect may reduce new infections. Pick off dead buds when they are seen.

Rhododendron powdery mildew

Powdery mildew can appear in winter or spring and discolours leaves. A feint fungal growth on the lower surface corresponds with red or yellow blotches on the upper leaf. Ensuring the plant has plenty of water and spraying it with products that are effective against powdery mildew will help.

Climbers

When a well-loved climber begins to ail, or a newly planted specimen unexpectedly dies, the first reaction is often one of bafflement. Establishing the cause is not always easy, but here are some common complaints.

See also:
• General pests and diseases on trees, shrubs, and climbers (*pp.66–69*)
• Know your enemy: pests and diseases (*pp.26–43*)

Earwig on clematis
Earwigs (*see p.31*) hide away during the day in dark crevices and then emerge at night when they eat the petals and young foliage of clematis and many other plants. They are active from spring to autumn. Earwigs can be trapped in pots loosely stuffed with dry grass, or spray plants at dusk with an insecticide containing bifenthrin.

Clematis slime flux
Affected clematis shoots become covered with a foul smelling cream, pink, or orange slimy growth. The original cause of most slime fluxes is a wound through which some of the plant's sap escapes. The stem often dies above this point. There are no chemical controls and it is best to cut back the stem below this wound, removing the diseased tissue.

Clematis wilt
Clematis wilt is caused by the fungus *Phoma clematidina*. Leaves and shoots of clematis wilt and die rapidly, although recovery is possible from healthy tissue either below soil level or from nodes that are beneath the wilted area. The wilt usually starts at the tips of the shoots, followed by blackening of the leaf stalks leading to wilting. Affected growth should be cut back to clean tissue, even if this is below ground level. Plant clematis in a deep and fertile soil in a moist and shaded area to encourage good root growth, which will subsequently help combat wilt. Large flowered hybrids are most susceptible to clematis wilt. Clematis species, including *C. montana*, are resistant and *C. viticella* is tolerant of infection.

Ivy leaf spot
Various fungi cause brown or grey spots on ivy foliage and, on variegated leaves, leaf spot is usually at its most acute on the white or pale areas. It doesn't usually affect the plant's vigour. Clip severely affected branches to help prevent the leaf spot from spreading, and, if possible, spray with fungicides that are used for other diseases on ornamentals.

Honeysuckle aphid

Dense colonies of greyish green aphids develop on the shoot tips and flower buds in late spring to early summer. Flower buds may be killed and the foliage is discoloured and distorted. A sticky honeydew is excreted by the aphids and this allows sooty moulds to grow. Spray the aphids when seen with thiacloprid, acetamiprid, bifenthrin, or pyrethrum.

Honeysuckle powdery mildew

Typically, a powdery white coating appears on the leaves, infected tissue becomes distorted, and leaves may drop. Outbreaks are most severe in dry soil conditions, so water regularly and also remove infected tissues to reduce further spread. Encourage air circulation by pruning. Spraying with myclobutanil, penconazole, or triticonazole may also help.

Wisteria die-back

While a soil-borne disease such as honey fungus, Phytophthora root rot, or Verticillium wilt (see pp.42–43) can be responsible for die-back, sudden wilting may, in fact, be because wisterias are grafted near ground level and graft failure may occur after many years. If this is the case, a new wisteria can be planted in the same position.

Wisteria scale

This is an unusually large, blackish brown scale, up to 10mm (½in) in diameter. First found in Britain in 2001, it mainly occurs in the London area, but will spread. It sucks sap from the stems of wisteria, *Prunus* and *Acer* species, sometimes causing die-back. On plants small enough to be sprayed, apply thiacloprid or acetamiprid in early summer.

Passion flower viruses

Passiflora can show typical symptoms of viruses. These include leaf distortion, yellowing, and leaf mottling. When grown indoors, they may be infected by common viruses occurring in glasshouses (see p.139). There are no cures and it is best to destroy plants showing symptoms if these persist. Sterilize tools and wash hands when handling infected plants.

Roses

Pests and diseases are the bane of rose growers, from greenfly infestations to black spot. Good cultivation and hygiene can reduce some problems, and most modern roses have been bred for their resistance to disease.

See also:
• General pests and diseases on trees, shrubs, and climbers (pp.66–69)
• Know your enemy: pests and diseases (pp.26–43), most specifically leaf-cutting bees (p.31), downy and powdery mildews (p.40), and honey fungus (p.43), which especially affect roses

Large rose sawfly larvae
The yellow and black females insert eggs into soft young rose stems in early and late summer. The pale green larvae are marked with black spots and yellow blotches. They feed gregariously and can rapidly defoliate the stems before going down into the soil to pupate. Remove the larvae by hand or spray with pyrethrum, bifenthrin, or thiacloprid.

Rose aphid
Several species of greenfly or aphids suck sap from the foliage, shoot tips, and flower buds during the spring and summer. Heavy infestations cause stunted growth and poor flowering. White cast aphid skins, honeydew, and sooty mould disfigure the plants. Spray infestations early with pyrethrum, bifenthrin, thiacloprid, or acetamiprid.

Rose leaf-rolling sawfly
The small black females lay eggs in rose leaflets, causing them to curl downwards and form leaf rolls. After hatching, the pale green caterpillar-like larva eats the rolled leaf. There is one generation in late spring to early summer. Remove rolled leaflets to prevent the larvae completing their feeding. Spraying with thiacloprid may give some control.

Rose slugworm sawfly
The pale green, semi-transparent caterpillar-like larvae, up to 15mm (⅝in) long, graze away the lower leaf surface, causing the damaged area to dry up and become whitish brown. There are two generations, with damage occurring in early and late summer. If necessary, control by spraying the slugworms with pyrethrum, bifenthrin, or thiacloprid.

Robin's pin cushion
Hard swellings, up to the size of a golf ball, develop in late summer on the stems of wild roses, sucker growth, and some garden species roses. These galls are covered in moss-like reddish yellow modified leaves. The gall is induced by small white grubs that develop inside the structure. No real damage is caused so control is unnecessary.

Rose leafhopper

A coarse, pale mottling develops on the upper leaf surface where the insect sucks sap from the underside of leaves, especially on roses in sheltered places. Adult rose leafhoppers are pale yellow and 3mm (⅛in) long and jump off the plant when disturbed. Control with thiacloprid, acetamiprid, bifenthrin, or pyrethrum if a damaging infestation is developing.

Rose black spot

Dark brown or black blotches appear on leaves from late spring onwards and affected leaves fall prematurely, which can weaken the plant. Encouraging vigorous growth will help plants. Initial infection is mainly from spots on stems in which the fungus *Diplocarpon rosae* has overwintered. Severe spring pruning to remove this tissue helps, as does thorough leaf clearance in autumn and mulching in spring. Various fungicides are available to help kill the fungus, and alternating applications of different active ingredients will find the most effective product. First spray immediately after spring pruning, and then spray once again when the leaves open.

Rose canker and die-back

Various fungi can cause canker and die-back of rose stems. Most infect the plant through bad pruning cuts or wounds. It is also important to plant roses so their graft union is not covered by soil and make clean pruning cuts close above a bud. To discourage die-back, feed with proprietary rose fertilizers and avoid drought or waterlogging.

Rose viruses

Several viruses are recorded on roses causing vein clearing, yellow flecking, or mottling on the leaves. The markings may be mild and not as clear as on other plants, but leaves may also be distorted and plants stunted as a result of the viral infection. No cures are available for viruses and it is best to destroy plants (*see also p.41*).

Rose rust

In spring, elongate patches of rust appear on stems and leaf stalks, followed by small bright orange dusty spots on the undersides of leaves, which turn brown by late summer. Often plants suffer severe defoliation. The spores overwinter on plant debris, soil, and stems. Cut out lesions on stems and destroy fallen leaves. Fungicides are available.

The herbaceous garden

The flower beds in a garden provide colour from spring to autumn. Even when most of the annuals, bulbs, and perennial herbaceous plants have died down at the end of the growing season, some still have foliage and seed heads to provide interest into autumn and beyond. Most gardens also have a lawn, and this expanse of mown grass between the beds needs to be kept in a healthy state if it is to provide a pleasing effect that enhances the floral display. Regular inspections will keep plants at their best by allowing for early detection of problems and their timely treatment.

Herbaceous plants: general pests and diseases

Herbaceous perennial plants, bulbs, and annuals can suffer from a wide range of pests and diseases, some of which can kill or seriously disfigure the plants.

Inspect plants at regular intervals so that signs of poor health or pest activity are detected in time for appropriate treatment.

The plant divisions in this chapter are:
- Perennials (*see pp.92–97*)
- Annuals (*see pp.98–99*)
- Bulbs, corms, tubers, and rhizomes (*see pp.100–103*)
- Lawns (*see pp.104–105*)

Swift moth caterpillars These live in the soil and feed on roots. They have brown heads and slender white bodies up to 50mm (2in) long, with three pairs of short legs at the head end and five pairs of clasper legs on the abdomen.

Tortrix moth caterpillars Pale green and up to 18mm (¾in) long, tortrix moth caterpillars bind two leaves together with silk threads and graze away the inner surfaces. Damaged areas dry up and turn brown. Many herbaceous plants and shrubs are attacked.

There is no effective insecticide control for swift moth caterpillars, but a pathogenic nematode is available from biocontrol suppliers.

The hidden nature of tortrix moth caterpillars makes control difficult with sprays. One non-chemical control is to squeeze the bound up leaves to crush the caterpillars. As well as attacking plants in the garden, they are problems in glasshouses (*see p.138*).

Southern green shield bug The southern green shield bug is currently found in the London area, but this sap-sucking bug is likely to spread further afield. The all-green, shield-shaped adult bugs and their spotty nymphs feed on beans, peas, tomatoes, raspberries, and many ornamental plants in late summer. The adults are up to 15mm (⅝in) long.

Leaf and bud eelworms These microscopic worm-like nematodes live inside the foliage of penstemon, Japanese anemones, chrysanthemums, and many other plants. They cause blackish brown discoloured areas in the leaves, which are often sharply divided from uninfested parts by the larger leaf veins. Damage is mainly seen in late summer to autumn.

Powdery mildew This fungus infects many herbaceous plants and the main ones that are affected are covered in their appropriate groups on the following pages. Symptoms include a powdery white coating appearing on any part of the plant and infected tissue becoming distorted. If it takes a hold, the leaves subsequently may drop, buds die, or stems die back.

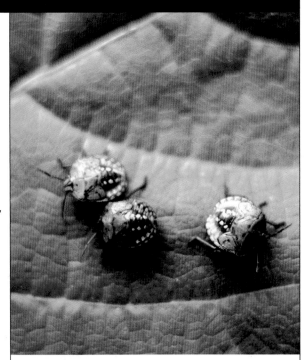

If necessary, southern green shield bugs can be controlled by spraying them with pyrethrum or bifenthrin.

There is no chemical control for leaf and bud eelworms. Dig out heavily infested plants.

Thin out shoots to improve air circulation, which helps reduce the incidence of disease. Fungicide sprays will also help.

Perennials

On perennials, pests and diseases may come and go, or they may be a persistent problem, such as hollyhock rust.

If you have damage on:
- Auriculas, see root aphid (*p.33*)
- Cineraria, gerbera, or marguerite daisies, see chrysanthemum leaf miner (*p.95*)
- Freesias or gladioli, see canna viruses (*p.97*)
- Lavatera, see hollyhock rust (*p.97*)
- Verbascum, see figwort weevil (*p.79*) as well as mullein moth (*below*)

See also:
- General pests and diseases on herbaceous plants (*pp.90–91*)
- Know your enemy: pests and diseases (*pp.26–43*)

Phlox eelworm
The microscopic worm-like eelworms or nematodes live inside the stems and foliage. Infested plants are stunted with abnormally swollen stems and foliage at the shoot tips, greatly reduced in width. Such stems often rot off. There is no chemical treatment so destroy infested plants. Put replacement plants in a different part of the garden.

Phormium mealybug
This greyish white sap-sucking insect lives in the folded bases of the leaves on New Zealand flax. It secretes a white waxy powder from its body. Heavily infested plants lack vigour and suffer die-back. There is no treatment because of difficulties in reaching the pest with an insecticide. Inspect new plants carefully to ensure you are not also buying the pest.

Sempervivum leaf miner
House leeks are damaged by the larvae of a leaf-mining hoverfly. Two generations occur in early and late summer, when the larvae hollow out the leaves in the outer portion of the rosettes, causing them to rot or dry up. Remove infested leaves when they are detected or treat pot-grown plants with a compost drench of thiacloprid or acetamiprid.

Mullein moth
The caterpillars are up to 48mm (1¾in) long and greyish white with black spots and yellow blotches. They eat the foliage and flowers of verbascums and sometimes buddleia in early to midsummer. When they have completed their feeding, they go into the soil to pupate. Remove the caterpillars by hand when seen or spray with pyrethrum or bifenthrin.

Solomon's seal sawfly
Greyish white caterpillar-like larvae, up to 25mm (1in) long, devour the foliage on Solomon's seal in early summer. Plants can be reduced to bare stems. There is one generation a year and the fully fed larvae go into the soil to overwinter. Look for holes appearing in the foliage and either pick off the larvae or spray with pyrethrum, bifenthrin, or thiacloprid.

Water lily beetle

Both the greyish brown beetles and their black grubs are up to 8mm (³⁄₈in) long. They live on the upper surface of water lily leaves where they eat out elongate slots. This damage encourages rotting and discolouration of the leaves. Insecticides cannot be used because of the danger to fish and other pondlife, so remove the beetles and larvae by hand if possible.

Water lily aphid

In summer, the upper surface of water lily leaves and the flower buds can be covered with brownish green aphids that are about 2mm (¹⁄₁₂in) long and their white cast skins. If the infestation is great, plant growth and flowering can be poor. Other floating pond plants may also be attacked. The aphids overwinter as eggs on plums and cherries, feeding on their young foliage before moving to water lillies in early summer. In late summer, the aphids migrate back to their winter host plants to lay eggs. Insecticides cannot be used against this pest as all pesticides are dangerous to fish and other pond wildlife. Instead, wipe aphids off the foliage and flower buds, or use a strong jet of water to blast them off.

Violet gall midge

Several generations of this tiny fly lay eggs on the developing leaves of violets during the spring and summer. Infested leaves fail to unfurl and are greatly swollen, and orange white maggots develop under the curled leaf margins. Plants generally survive this pest and still produce growth and flowers. This is fortunate as there is no effective control.

Michaelmas daisy mite

It is mainly *Aster novi-belgii* that is affected by these microscopic mites, which live in the shoot tips and flower buds where they suck sap. This causes stunted growth with scarring on the stems. Flowers are converted into rosettes of small leaves with no petals. There is no treatment so dispose of infested plants. *Aster novae-angliae* and *A. amellus* are not damaged.

Geum sawfly

Pale green larvae, up to 15mm (⁵⁄₈in) long, with forked spines on their upper surface devour the young leaves of geums in late spring to early summer. Leaves can be stripped to the central veins. Remove caterpillars by hand or spray with thiacloprid, bifenthrin, or pyrethrum. If the plants are in flower, use insecticides in the evening to avoid harming bees.

Perennials *continued*

Geranium sawfly
From late spring to the end of summer, the foliage of hardy geraniums develops holes made by the caterpillar-like sawfly larvae. They are greyish green with black heads and are up to 11mm (½in) long. Two or three generations occur over the summer. Only control if the leaves are being severely holed. Spray with thiacloprid, bifenthrin, or pyrethrum.

Geranium powdery mildew
Symptoms of white powdery coating are seen on both the upper and lower surfaces of geranium leaves and are caused by several species of fungi. Improving air circulation by pruning and making sure the roots are kept moist by watering during dry periods, together with mulching in the spring, go some way towards reducing the infection.

Pelargonium rust
This rust causes yellow blotches on the upper leaves corresponding to a ring of brown pustules on the lower surfaces. In severe attacks, both surfaces may be infected. Leaves turn yellow and fall, weakening the plant to the point it may die. Destroy badly infected leaves or plants. Improve ventilation and spray with fungicide labelled for control of rusts.

Lupin aphid
Greyish white aphids, up to 4mm (⅛in) long, form dense colonies on the underside of lupin leaves and on the flower spikes. Plants become sticky with honeydew excreted by the pest. In heavy attacks, the plant may wilt and die. Check lupins for signs of infestation during the spring and, if necessary, spray with thiacloprid, acetamiprid, bifenthrin, or pyrethrum.

Lupin anthracnose
This is a serious fungal disease of lupins. Large lesions develop on the stems or leaves, which can then lead to rapid collapse. Sometimes pink spores are also evident within the diseased tissue. Affected plants should be removed and destroyed. The fungus can be seed-borne. No fungicide is currently available to control this disease.

Hemerocallis gall midge
Eggs are laid on daylily buds during late spring to early summer. Many tiny maggots feed inside the buds, making them abnormally swollen and squat, and they dry up or rot without opening. There are no insecticide treatments so destroy galled buds before the larvae complete their feeding. Cultivars flowering after mid-July escape damage.

Chrysanthemum leaf miner
This tiny fly has larvae that make narrow twisting white or brown tunnels (or mines) in the foliage of chrysanthemums, cinerarias, gerberas, marguerite daisies, and other related plants. Several generations a year occur on indoor plants. For light infestations, pick off affected parts of leaves, otherwise spraying with thiacloprid or acetamiprid may control the larvae.

Chrysanthemum white rust
White rust is a relatively new disease, but is now more widespread than brown rust (*right*). It has dirty white pustules on the lower leaf surface with corresponding pale craters on the upper leaf. Destroy affected plants and neighbouring chrysanthemums and do not propagate from them. Spray with a fungicide for control of rusts on ornamentals.

Chrysanthemum brown rust
Brown rust appears in late summer, although many cultivars are now resistant. Dark brown pustules on the underside of leaves correspond with pale green spots on the upper surface. It can cause defoliation and a reduction in flowering. Destroy diseased material and strip lower leaves from cuttings when taken and transplanted. Use fungicides for control of rusts.

Delphinium black botch
This bacterial disease starts on delphinium leaves, but then spreads to the plant's stems and flowers. The bacteria are splashed from the soil and infect through the leaves to cause large black blotches. No chemicals are labelled to control this disease so all that remains is to destroy badly affected plants as soon as possible.

Delphinium powdery mildew
Delphiniums are particularly prone to powdery mildew, especially in hot summers. The symptoms are a white powdery coating on the leaves and stems. To help control, avoid overcrowding, destroy infected plant material, and spray with an appropriate fungicide. Delphinium Pacific Hybrids Series might be resistant to this disease.

Dianthus smut
The symptoms of dianthus smut are stunting of the flower stalks and distortion of the anthers, which are filled with spores of the fungus *Microbotryum dianthorum*. The fungus probably occurs throughout the plant so do not take cuttings and destroy the affected plants before the buds open. Rest the soil for at least five years before re-planting.

Perennials *continued*

Peony wilt
A common fungal disease of peonies is caused by the fungus *Botrytis paeoniae*. In spring or early summer, shoots may wilt and die. A grey fluffy mould can be seen on brown areas at the stem base, and brown blotches appear on leaves, particularly at their tips. The fungus produces air-borne spores and sclerotia, which can remain dormant in the soil, so it is important to promptly cut back affected tissue, if necessary to below soil level. This material should not be composted and the soil around the crown of the plant needs to be replaced. The disease thrives in humid conditions, so peony clumps must not become too dense. No fungicides are currently available that will control this disease.

Acanthus powdery mildew
White powdery coating is seen on the upper surfaces of the leaves. Once established, acanthus can become very densely planted, so to help prevent the disease, thin out the plants as much as possible, cut out infected material, and only water around the roots. Spraying with an appropriate fungicide such as myclobutanil, penconazole, and triticonazole may help.

Hellebore black death
Black death is a viral disease that causes the blackening and severe distortion of hellebore leaves and flowers. In early stages, black streaks are evident in leaf and sepal veins. It cannot be eradicated and is not well understood. Dig up affected plants and burn them. Spray neighbours with an aphicide to reduce the risk of being infected by hellebore aphid.

Hellebore leaf blotch
Hellebore leaf spot is caused by the fungus *Microsphaeropsis hellebori*. Large brown spots appear on the leaves, which eventually become silvery. In severe cases, the whole leaf may die, weakening the remaining plant. Sometimes flower stems and the hellebore flowers may be affected, resulting in the stems drooping. Infection can occur very rapidly under appropriate damp conditions. Removal of the previous year's foliage before the emergence of flowers will reduce the inoculum that overwinters. Even if you end up removing a lot of the leaves from the hellebore plant, they should soon regenerate. Destroy affected material promptly. Myclobutanil, penconazole, and triticonazole may give some control.

Hollyhock rust

The hollyhock rust fungus (*Puccinia malvacearum*) also attacks *Lavatera* and related genera. The fungus attacks all green parts of the plant, but is most noticeable as conspicuous yellow or orange spots on the upper leaves and bracts with corresponding orange pustules on the lower surfaces. These may fuse together eventually, leading to the collapse of portions of leaves, leaving them looking unsightly and ragged. The spores are wind dispersed and the fungus can survive during mild winters on infected leaves and plant debris. No resistant hollyhock is known but *Althea rugosa* might be less susceptible. The plants should be sprayed regularly using a fungicide labelled for rusts.

Periwinkle rust

In addition to the usual rust symptoms (*see p.41*), affected plants often fail to produce flowers, develop an erect habit, and may distort. The fungus can permeate the rootstock so any diseased plants must be uprooted and destroyed. Since the fungus is perennial, the fungicides available to control rust diseases are of limited use.

Canna viruses

Cannas can be affected by several viruses: canna yellow mottle (affects only canna), the new canna yellow streak (little is known) or bean yellow mosaic, which infects many plants, including beans, peas, freesias, and gladioli. The symptoms on canna are usually small chlorotic spots over the leaves. There are no chemical controls; destroy the affected plants.

Antirrhinum rust

The symptoms of antirrhinum rust are small, dark brown pustules on the undersides of leaves, with a corresponding pale dimple on the upper surface. In severe attacks leaves shrivel and die and plants are badly damaged. Spread by airborne spores, the fungus *Puccinia antirrhini* also has an overwintering spore. This rarely happens, however, and most carry-over is on plants that are kept from one season to another. Cultivars claimed to resist rust are available, but with different strains of the fungus developing, rust may still affect them. Regular sprays with a fungicide labeled to control rusts can be used. Destroy plants at the end of the season to avoid carry-over of fungal spores.

Annuals

We set great store by annuals, whether they are bedding plants from the garden centre or flowers nurtured from seed. So it is infuriating if a pest or disease threatens your hopes for a garden bounty.

If you have damage on:
- Cineraria, gerbera, or marguerite daisy, see chrysanthemum leaf miner (*p.95*)

See also:
- General pests and diseases on herbaceous plants (*pp.90–91*)
- Know your enemy: pests and diseases (*pp.26–43*)

Cabbage white caterpillars on nasturtiums
Nasturtiums can be defoliated by caterpillars of the large cabbage white butterfly and, like brassicas, can also fall prey to the small cabbage white buterfly (*see p.115*) during the summer. The hairy caterpillars are up to 40mm (1½in) long and pale yellow with black mottling. There are two generations a year, with the hairy caterpillars appearing from spring to early autumn. The best way to control them is to remove them by hand, but if they are too numerous to control in this way, spray with an insecticide such as pyrethrum or bifenthrin. If the nasturtiums are in flower, spray them in the evening to avoid harming bees.

Impatiens downy mildew
The downy mildew that infects *Impatiens* (*Plasmopara obducens*) was introduced in the UK in 2003. The disease is so far confined to *Impatiens walleriana* (busy Lizzie), but all members of the family may be at risk. Thes symptoms are that the leaves turn yellow and shed from the plant. It is often then reduced to bare branches and may die. Furthermore, fine white fungal growth may be visible on the lower leaf surface. To help prevent infection, space plants reasonably well apart, avoid overhead irrigation, and apply a general fertilizer. Affected plants should be disposed of immediately and not composted to avoid risk of further contamination. Rest affected areas from *Impatiens* for several years.

Sweet pea powdery mildew
A white powdery coating develops on leaves. It is first seen as discrete off-white patches, which may later spread on the plant. The leaves may turn yellow and die. To help prevent the problem, make sure the roots do not dry out and improve ventilation by spacing or clipping plants. You can also use fungicides approved for powdery mildew on ornamentals.

Pansy downy mildew

The symptoms of pansy downy mildew are brown-purple spots on upper leaf surfaces, usually with a surrounding yellow halo corresponding with mould on the underside. Badly affected plants shrivel and become debilitated or die. Remove infected leaves promptly and destroy infected plants if they become badly affected.

Pansy leaf spots

Two fungi cause dark and pale leaf spots on pansies, and a further fungus causes black leaf blotches and crown rot. Spores are produced on the undersides of the leaves and are spread by water splash. The fungi can contaminate the soil for several years. Rotate plants and fungicides that are labelled for other ornamental diseases may give control.

Pansy sickness

Pansy sickness is a term loosely used to describe foot and stem rot problems occurring on pansies. The foliage dies and eventually the plant is killed. Several soil-borne fungi can cause these symptoms, including species of *Pythum*. Destroy infected plants. Improving drainage and applying a rotation will reduce pathogen build-up in the soil.

Nicotiana downy mildew

The symptoms of the downy mildew that affects *Nicotiana* are yellow patches on the leaves corresponding with blue mould on the undersides. The disease spreads during the season by wind-blown spores and persists in the soil as resistant spores for an unknown length of time. Destroy the infected plants and then avoid replanting.

Nicotiana viruses

Tobacco is host for many viruses, including tobacco mosaic virus and tobacco necrosis virus. Symptoms include yellow mottling, spotting, and mosaics, and can also feature distortion and stunted growth. Destroy all infected plants as there are no cures, and ensure that you wash your hands, sterilize tools, and use fresh soil.

Petunia viruses

Petunias can be affected by several viruses. Typical symptoms are yellow flecks and spots, mosaics, and streaks on the foliage. The plants may also be stunted. Destroy all affected plants immediately as there is no cure for viruses. You must always wash your hands thoroughly and sterilize tools both before and after handling petunias.

Bulbs, corms, tubers, and rhizomes

Sometimes pests and diseases of these plants are plain to see, such as lily beetle, but if problems occur underground or during a plants' dormant phase, you may not be aware until it is too late.

If you have damage on:
• *Hemerocallis* and gladioli, see iris leaf spot (*opposite*)

See also:
• General pests and diseases on herbaceous plants (*pp.90–91*)
• Know your enemy: pests and diseases (*pp.26–43*)

Gladiolus thrips
These are yellowish white as immature nymphs but black when adult. They have narrow elongate bodies up to 2mm ($^1/_{12}$ in) long and suck sap, causing a pale mottling of the foliage and flowers, which may fail to open. Spray with acetamiprid or thiacloprid when signs of damage are seen. Dispose of or burn dead tops to get rid of overwintering thrips.

Bulb scale mite
Hippeastrum and narcissus bulbs forced for early flowering indoors are susceptible to this pest. The microscopic mites live in the neck of the bulbs where they suck sap causing scarring along the edges of the leaves and flower stems. Growth is stunted, with leaves having a curved appearance. There is no effective treatment, so discard infested bulbs.

Lily beetle
Both the adults and grubs of the lily beetle eat the foliage of lilies and fritillaries. The adult beetle is 8mm ($^3/_8$in) long and bright red with black legs and head. The grubs are reddish brown with black heads. The grubs are often completely covered with their own wet, black excrement.Lily beetle damage occurs from spring until early autumn. In addition to eating the leaves, the beetles and grubs also damage the flowers and seedpods. Lily beetle used to be confined to south-east England, but now occurs throughout Britain. To control the pest, remove the beetles and grubs by hand or spray the affected plants with thiacloprid or acetamiprid as soon as damage is noticed.

Lily disease
With lily disease, the fungus *Botrytis elliptica* causes elliptical, water-soaked spots, which appear on the leaves and may enlarge to rot the entire leaf and spread to the stem or flowers. Affected growth must be removed and burnt. Good air circulation among leaves will reduce the disease's incidence. No fungicides are available to treat this disease.

Iris ink disease

The fungus *Drechslera iridis* causes black patches and streaks on the exterior of bulbs and the foliage shows yellow streaks. The leaves may turn red-brown and wither or turn black after emergence. The fungus persists on overwintered infected bulbs, crop debris, and possibly on soil. Remove affected bulbs and grow in a fresh position.

Iris rust

The fungus *Puccinia iridis* causes pale leaf spots bearing brown or black slit-like pustules and the leaves may subsequently wither and die. Older leaves are usually the most badly affected. The alternate host for the fungus is probably nettles. Cut off the worst affected leaves and use an approved rust fungicide to help to control the disease.

Anemone smut

The cause of anemone smut is the fungus *Urocystis*. Dark streaks and blisters appear on the leaves and stems of anemones, creeping buttercups, and globeflowers. These burst to release spores, which can persist in plant debris. There are no chemical controls, but removal of the affected parts may limit spread. Rest soil from host plants for several years.

Iris sawfly

Only waterside irises, such as *Iris pseudacorus*, *I. ensata*, *I. spuria*, *I. versicolor*, and *I. laevigata* are susceptible. Greyish brown, caterpillar-like larvae, up to 25mm (1in) long, eat the foliage in midsummer and may cause severe defoliation. Avoid using insecticides near ponds because of the danger to fish and other pondlife. Remove the sawfly larvae by hand.

Iris leaf spot

This fungal leaf spot also affects related plants such as *Hemerocallis* and gladioli. On rhizomatous irises, brown spots with yellow margins develop; bulbous irises display grey spots without a border. Leaves may die, usually after flowering. It is worst in wet years or on wet soils. Cut back diseased leaves. Fungicides labelled for use on ornamentals may help.

Mouse and squirrel damage

Squirrels and mice dig up and eat some bulbs and corms, especially crocuses and tulips. Such plants are particularly vulnerable in the first year after planting. The bulb or corm is eaten while the foliage is left lying on the soil. Tread the ground down firmly after planting to disguise the locations of new plantings. See pages 36–37 for the limited control options.

Bulbs, corms, tubers, and rhizomes *continued*

Narcissus smoulder

This foliar disease becomes evident when the newly emerged shoots show infected tips bearing a grey mass of spores. The lesions can also be produced on one margin of the leaf. Affected leaves and flower stalks die back. Remove infected leaves, destroy bulbs on which the resting structures of the fungus (sclerotia) can be seen, and clear up leaf debris.

Narcissus eelworm

The microscopic nematodes live inside the bulb and foliage. Infested plants are stunted and the bulbs rot. If an infested bulb is cut transversely in half, concentric brown rings can be seen. There is no effective control. Remove infested plants and any other narcissus growing within 1m (39in). Buy good-quality bulbs to avoid introducing this pest into a garden.

Narcissus bulb fly

Daffodils, snowdrops, and *Hippeastrum* bulbs are damaged by plump, creamy white maggots, up to 18mm (¾in) long, that eat out the centre. Damaged bulbs often rot or produce just a few thin leaves. There are no effective controls. Growing the plants in shaded places reduces the number of eggs that are laid as the adult fly prefers warm sunny places.

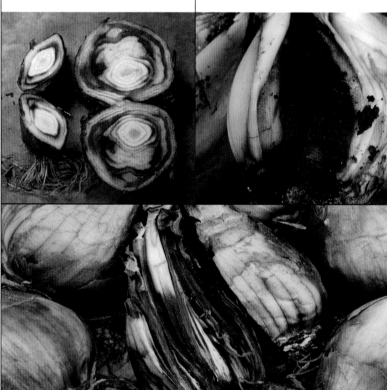

Narcissus basal rot

Basal rot is one of the most serious diseases of *Narcissus*. It is most common in hot summers when the bulbs are dying back naturally. Lifted bulbs begin to rot after a month, the basal plate becomes soft, and a red rot spreads through the inner scales, sometimes with a pink mould present. Bulbs in the soil will rot and the disease spread to neighbours. The fungus is thought to invade through the roots, possibly via wounds, from adhering soil. Lifting bulbs in June and storing in a cool, airy place may reduce disease development. Also, it is worth inspecting bulbs and removing those that are soft. The Triandrus, Jonquil, and Tazetta groups of narcissus are resistant to basal rot disease.

Narcissus white mould

This fungal foliar disease causes elongate yellowing lesions near the tips of the leaves on which a grey white fungus can be seen. Affected leaves die back, reducing the yield of bulbs and flowers. It produces black resting structures that eventually fall in the soil. The fungus is not carried on the bulb. Maintain good hygiene and plant narcissus in a fresh place.

Narcissus leaf scorch

This fungal disease affects the tips of emerging leaves, which develop reddish brown scorching that may spread down the leaves. They turn yellow and shrivel, and brown blotches may appear on the flowers. Remove the affected tissue promptly to limit the disease spread. Avoid storing the bulbs at low temperatures or planting late.

Tulip fire

Brown scorching deforms the young shoots. Sunken yellow spots with green halos appear on the leaves of neighbours. In humid conditions, the fungus shows up as a grey mould on the affected tissue. Inspect bulbs before planting for small black bodies within lesions. Destroy affected plants as spread is rapid. Avoid growing tulips in affected soil for three years.

Snowdrop grey mould

This fungal disease is usually worst in mild winters. Growth is stunted and leaves and flower stalk rot. Diseased tissue is sometimes covered with grey, velvety fungal growth. Small black sclerotia may develop on the bulb, which rots. Dig up infected clumps and do not replant there for as long as possible. Examine bulbs before planting for the small black sclerotia.

Storage rots

Narcissus bulbs are prone to a variety of bulb rots, sometimes exacerbated by unsuitable storage conditions. Lilies and irises are prone to bulb rots where infection leads to a soft rot and a mass of blue/green spores, which usually enter through wounds. Store only perfect bulbs in a cool, shaded, well-ventilated place. Avoid damaging bulbs through handling.

Dahlia smut

Circular or elliptical leaf spots arise, which enlarge, darken, and merge, but usually retain a yellow margin. The symptoms spread upwards. The fungus persists as spores in the soil, but transmission does not occur in seeds or tubers. Dispose of diseased foliage in the autumn and remove leaves close to the tubers before storing. Rest soil for at least five years.

Lawns

If you are looking for a perfect lawn, it is to your benefit to be knowledgeable of the various pests, diseases, and cultural problems that may stand in your way. These vary from the well known – moles and fairy rings – to the more stealthy, like red thread and snow mould.

See also:
- Know your enemy: pests and diseases (*pp.26–43*)
- Pathogenic nemotodes (*p.63*)

Moles

Moles feed on earthworms and soil insects that enter the network of underground tunnels that each mole creates. This results in molehills where soil has been excavated onto the surface, and unevenness in the lawn surface when tunnels collapse. Mole deterrent devices are available but they are not infallible. Mole traps are more reliable (*see p.57*).

Burrowing bees

Some species of solitary bees, such as *Andrena* spp., dig their nest tunnels in short turf. They are mainly active in spring when the female bees dig out vertical tunnels topped by a small conical heap of excavated soil. No damage is caused by this digging and since solitary bees are useful pollinating insects, they should be tolerated rather than eliminated.

Chafer grubs

These curved beetle larvae, up to 18mm (¾in) long, eat grass roots. The species most frequently associated with lawn damage are Welsh chafer and garden chafer. Badgers, foxes, and crows rip up the loose turf in autumn to spring to feed on the grubs. Treat lawns with imidacloprid in early summer, or apply a pathogenic nematode (*see p.63*).

Leatherjackets

Leatherjackets are the larvae of crane flies or daddy long-legs. The maggots feed on grass roots and can kill patches of lawns in late winter to summer. The thick-skinned larvae are greyish brown and up to 40mm (1½in) long. Control the young larvae with imidacloprid in early autumn or use a pathogenic nematode as a biological control (*see p.63*).

Ants

Ants in lawns are a nuisance rather than a damaging pest. They tunnel underground and bring soil onto the surface above the nest. This impedes mowing and can result in an uneven lawn surface, but little direct damage is done to the grass. Ant nests are difficult to eradicate and are best tolerated. Brush away any excavated soil to prevent mounds from forming.

Worm casts

Some species of earthworm produce a muddy excrement, known as worm casts, on the surface of lawns, mainly in autumn to spring. This makes the lawn look unsightly and more difficult to mow. Weed seeds are likely to germinate on worm casts. There are no chemicals available for worm control. Rake or brush worm casts when they are dry to disperse them.

Toadstools in turf

Many toadstools can appear in lawns especially following a disturbance that has increased the organic matter (fertilizing, weedkilling, scarifying). Most of these fungi (except for some types of fairy rings) are not killing the grass as they convert the organic matter into nutrients for plants. They can appear unsightly and picking them off is the only remedy.

Slime moulds

These harmless organisms often appear, coating blades of grass in late spring or early autumn. Their colour varies, but it is commonly white or yellow and they change into grey, spherical, spore-bearing structures. They are entirely superficial and no control measures are necessary. Their appearance is short-lived, but they can be easily washed away if desired.

Turf red thread

Fine turf is frequently affected by this fungal disease, mainly in late summer and autumn. Reddish patches of grass and pink gelatinous fungal structures appear. When dry, these can be easily spread by foot. The grass usually recovers, but improving the aeration helps, as does use of high nitrogen fertilizers and the fungicide trifloxystrobin.

Turf fairy rings

Several fungi can disfigure lawns by forming fairy rings. The most serious form has an area of dead grass caused by the production of a dense mat of fungal growth in the soil. Spread may be halted by removing affected grass and soil to a depth of at least 30cm (12in), extending 30cm (12in) beyond the edge of the ring and replacing with fresh topsoil before reseeding.

Snow mould

Small patches of yellow, dying grass appear during mild, moist weather in spring or autumn. These turn brown and enlarge, and white or pink fungal growth may mat the blades of grass. Improve aeration, prune overhanging shrubs, and iron sulphate can reduce the disease's severity. Do not apply nitrogenous fertilizers after summer. Also try the fungicide trifloxystrobin.

The productive garden

Harvesting your own fruits and vegetables is something that is very satisfying for the gardener. However, nothing spoils this pleasure more than finding a crop of tomatoes or potatoes affected by blight, fruits damaged by maggots, and pea pods full of caterpillars. It is best to try to prevent conditions that favour problems. Identifying the cause is the first step to a cure. Once identified, treat the problem promptly before it spreads. Sometimes the damage is done before you can do anything about it, but steps can be taken to prevent pests and diseases from occurring again in the future.

Vegetables: general pests and diseases

It is a distressing sight to see a whole crop of vegetables destroyed in the garden. With good cultivation techniques and protective measures, losses can be kept to a minimum. The key is to be able to spot problems early and deal with them promptly before they become overwhelming.

The vegetable divisions in this chapter are:
- Peas and beans (*see pp.112–113*)
- Brassicas (*see pp.114–115*)
- Potatoes and parsnips (*see pp.116–117*)
- Salad crops (*see pp.118–119*)
- Assorted vegetables (*see pp.120–121*)

Cutworms These are brownish white caterpillars of various moth species. They live in the surface layers of the soil and eat cavities in root crops and potato tubers. They also kill seedlings and lettuce by eating through the roots.

Wireworms Click beetle larvae grow into wireworms and are mainly a problem in new gardens. The slender, orange-yellow grubs are up to 25mm (1in) long (*see p.33*), with three pairs of short legs at the head end. They kill seedlings and bore into potato tubers, onion bulbs, and other root vegetables. Numbers decline after a year or two.

Colorado beetle This beetle is a notifiable pest not found in Britain and Ireland, although widespread elsewhere in Europe. The beetle and its reddish brown

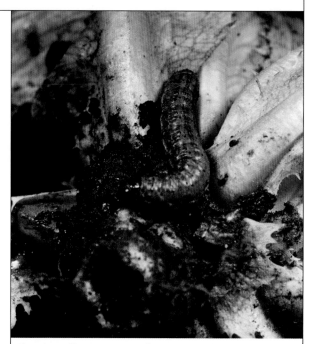

There is no effective treatment for cutworms – if a plant wilts, search through the soil around the plant and remove the pest.

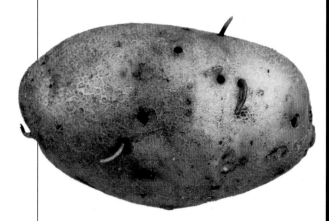

Wireworms bore holes in potato tubers, but there is no insecticide available for their control.

If you find a Colorado beetle or larva in Britain, keep it and report the location to the Plant Health and Seeds Inspectorate.

Honeybees use the holes made by bumblebees when nectar robbing to take nectar, so bypassing the pollination process.

grubs eat potato, tomato, aubergine, and pepper leaves, and may cause complete defoliation.

Nectar robbing Bees should visit the front of flowers, so they contact the pollen-bearing parts and transfer pollen to the stigma. Some bumblebees cheat and make shortcuts to the nectar in runner and broad bean flowers by biting holes in the back of the flowers. There is nothing that can be done about this.

Clubroot With this disease, plants become stunted and leaves may wilt on hot days, recovering overnight. The roots thicken and distort into a swollen mass. It can affect all crucifers and is usually introduced on seedlings brought into the garden. Improving drainage and liming the soil will help, as can raising seedlings in pots before planting them out in the garden.

White blister This disease is common on many crucifers. White chalky eruptions develop on the underside of leaves and distortion and discolouration may correspond on the upper surface. Although unsightly, white blister is not serious and the only control measure that is required is to remove affected leaves.

No chemicals are available to control clubroot, but various resistant brassica cultivars have been bred.

To reduce the incidence of white blister, space plants well and practise rotation (*see p.23*).

Fruit: general pests and diseases

Garden fruit is a sweet bounty, so it comes as no surprise that it is targeted by pests. Any incidence of disease should be taken seriously so these long-lived plants do not fail.

The fruit divisions in this chapter are:
- Fruit trees: apples and pears (*see pp.122–123*)
- Fruit trees: *Prunus* (*see pp.124–125*)
- Soft fruit (*see pp.126–127*)
- Raspberries and strawberries (*see pp.128–129*)

Brown scale This is a sap-sucking insect that lives on the stems of peaches, nectarines, grape vines, plums, and cane and bush fruits, as well as many ornamental shrubs. Mature females are covered by convex, oval, dark brown shells, up to 6mm (¼in) long.

Winter moth The adult moths emerge in early winter and lay eggs on apple, plum, cherry, and many other deciduous trees. The pale green looper caterpillars eat the foliage and blossom in spring before going into the soil to pupate. Prevent the wingless female moths climbing trunks by applying sticky grease bands in the autumn.

Spray a winter plant oil against brown scale overwintering nymphs, or spray in early summer with plant oils, fatty acids, or thiacloprid.

To control newly hatched winter moth caterpillars, spray them with bifenthrin at bud burst.

Protect fruit trees and bushes from bird damage by growing them in a fruit cage covered with wire or plastic netting (*see p.58*).

Bird damage Bullfinches can devour flower buds of fruit trees and bushes in winter. Blackbirds and other birds eat fruit berries and peck holes in apples, plums, and pears in the summer.

Fruit tree red spider mite This is a tiny, sap-sucking pest that lives on the underside of apple and plum foliage. Its feeding causes a fine pale mottling of the upper leaf surface. Heavy infestations can develop in hot summers, resulting in early leaf fall.

Blossom wilt Many fruit trees suffer from this disease, which is worst in damp springs. Usually the flowers wilt and turn brown, and the fungus that causes blossom wilt may grow into the spur to kill leaves or form cankers on branches. Spores are blown from overwintering infections to attack the flowers as they open. Spraying at this time may reduce disease incidence.

Fireblight This is a bacterial disease that affects apple-like plants in the *Rosaceae* family. It is a serious disease of pears, apples, and related ornamentals, such as *Cotoneaster*, *Pyracantha*, *Sorbus*, and hawthorn. It does not attack *Prunus* species. Leaves of affected branches wilt and brown, as if scorched by fire, and it can spread down the inner bark and result in sunken cankers.

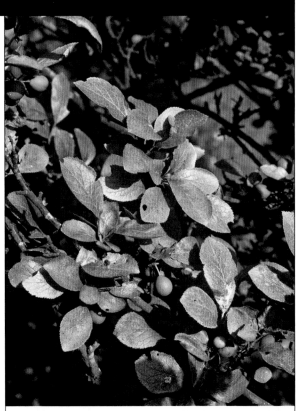

If red spider mite is seen on apples, spray with bifenthrin, plant oils, or fatty acids. On plums, use plant oils or fatty acids.

To control blossom wilt, cut out any diseased tissue in summer and remove fruit suffering from brown rot.

If a fruit tree becomes diseased by fireblight, swiftly prune the affected branches and sterilize tools.

Peas and beans

Usually easy to grow, and mostly trouble-free, peas and beans are a reliable garden crop. Pea moth and aphids are the most commonly seen, but be prepared to deal with other problems as well.

See also:
- General pests and diseases on vegetables (*pp.108–109*)
- Know your enemy: pests and diseases (*pp.26–43*)
- Potassium deficiency effects on beans (*p.15*)
- Canna viruses (*p.97*)
- Crop rotation (*p.23*)
- Barriers and repellents (*pp.58–59*)

Pea and bean weevil
The greyish brown beetles are 4–5mm (¹⁄₈–¹⁄₄in) long. They are active during the summer when they eat uniformly sized U-shaped notches from the leaf margins of broad bean and peas. Leaves may be extensively nibbled, but most of the leaf survives, so the impact on established plants is small. Seedling plants may need protection by spraying with bifenthrin or pyrethrum.

Pea moth
Eggs are laid on pea plants in early to midsummer. The caterpillars bore into the pods and feed on the developing pea seeds. Early or late sowings of quick maturing pea cultivars that flower outside the moth's flight period avoid damage. Mid-season peas can be given some protection by spraying with bifenthrin about a week after the onset of flowering.

Pea thrips
Thrips have narrow elongate bodies up to 2mm (¹⁄₁₂in) long. The adults are black but the nymphs are creamy yellow. They suck sap from the foliage and pods, causing a silvery brown discolouration. Heavy attacks can occur in hot summers. Damaged pods may contain only a few seeds. If necessary, spray with bifenthrin or pyrethrum when damage is seen.

Pea powdery mildew
The discolouration on the upper surfaces of leaves caused by powdery mildew associated with a white fungal film. It is favoured by dew formation. Severe infection reduces seed quality and impairs pea flavour. It survives on infected debris and may be seedborne. There are cultivars less susceptible to the disease. Early planting may help and use sulphur to control it.

Pea downy mildew
The fungus causes lesions on the upper surface of leaves corresponding to off-white mould on the underside. Infected pods turn brown and can distort. Tendrils become bleached. Infection at emergence causes the seedlings to be stunted and to die. There is no chemical control so remove infected plants and rest the soil from peas for several years.

Bean seed fly
The white maggots, up to 8mm (³⁄₈in) long, feed on germinating seeds of runner and French beans. If the seedlings survive, they may be blind as a result of the shoot tips being eaten. There are no insecticides available for this pest. Seedlings can be raised under cover in pots or trays for planting out after they are past the vulnerable germination stage.

Black bean aphid
As well as broad beans, this insect attacks French and runner beans in early to midsummer. Dense colonies develop on the shoot tips and leaves, resulting in a poor crop. Pinching out the tops of broad beans once four whorls of flowers have developed makes the plants less susceptible. If necessary, spray with pyrethrum, fatty acids, plant oils, or bifenthrin.

Bean rust
Dark brown pustules appear on leaves and pods of runner and French beans, and it can be more common in warm, damp summers. The white cluster-cup stage of the fungus may develop later in the season. There is no chemical control, so destroy affected tissue when seen. Avoid over-fertilizing as high nitrogen levels will increase bean susceptibility.

Bean chocloate spot
Chocolate spot is characterized by dark brown or grey spots on the leaves, petals, pods, and stems. Lesions can blacken, increase in size, and coalesce, leading to a destructive blight. The pathogen can overwinter in lesions. Remove infected plants. No fungicides are available. All commercial bean cultivars are at least moderately susceptible to the disease.

Bean halo blight
This is a seed-borne bacterial disease where water-soaked, angular lesions appear on leaves and pods. They coalesce, becoming brown, and there is a yellow halo around spots. Red streaks appear on stems. Leaves die, stems may be girdled, and seeds rot or remain immature. Destroy infected plants, choose resistant cultivars, and avoid overhead irrigation.

Bean anthracnose
Bean anthracnose is caused by a fungus that causes red-brown lesions on the leaves and veins. Lesions also appear on the stems and pods. Plants collapse and seeds may shrivel. It is primarily a seed-borne disease and survival on debris is limited. There is no chemical control. Use appropriate resistant cultivars as new races of the fungus continue to appear.

Brassicas and cabbages

Plants in the cabbage family are prone to a number of pests and diseases, so learn about the problems and plan accordingly. It will be necessary to protect crops from major pests like pigeons, caterpillars, or root fly.

See also:
- General pests and diseases on vegetables (*pp.108–109*)
- Know your enemy: pests and diseases (*pp.26–43*)
- Crop rotation (*p.23*)
- Barriers and repellents (*pp.58–59*)

Brassica flea beetles
All brassicas and allied plants, such as turnip, swede, radishes, and rocket, can be attacked by flea beetles. They are 2–3mm ($\frac{1}{12}$–$\frac{1}{8}$in) long and mostly black, sometimes with a yellow stripe down the wing cases. They eat small holes in the foliage and can kill seedlings. Encourage seedling growth by watering. If necessary, spray with bifenthrin, thiacloprid, or pyrethrum.

Brassica downy mildew
Yellow patches appear on the upper leaf surfaces with white fungal growth underneath the lesions of many brassicas. The disease is usually most severe on seedlings. Seeds may be infected. On radishes, black lesions on the root may be seen. Improve ventilation by spacing plants. Use resistant cultivars and rotate crops as the fungus can survive in the soil.

Brassica light leaf spot
The fungus *Cylindrosporium concentricum* causes large white blotches that contain small green flecks on very susceptible hosts, but symptoms may vary depending on weather conditions and host susceptibility. Lesions can appear on both the upper and lower surfaces of leaves. Early infection causes leaf distortion and stunting. Black spotting of the leaves and discolouration of the petioles can also occur, causing rotting of the leaves. Stems and pods can also be infected by the fungus. The disease is more severe with longer periods of leaf wetness and cool temperatures. Destroy infected plants, plant more tolerant cultivars, and practise crop rotation or leave two years between each brassica crop.

Brassica ring spot
Ring spot is caused by a fungus and is common in cool, wet areas. It causes dark spots with an angular appearance, often surrounded by a yellow halo, on leaves and pods. The entire leaf then turns yellow and, in severe infections, plants defoliate. Rotate with non-hosts, destroy all infected crop residues, and plant resistant cultivars.

Pigeon damage

Damage to brassicas by pigeons occurs at any time of year, but they are particularly troublesome in cold winters. They rip off pieces of leaf until plants are reduced to stalks. Shooting is not usually feasible, so protect plants by growing under a cage with netting. Scaring devices, such as scarecrows or humming tapes, do not give reliable protection.

Cabbage moth

The caterpillars are yellowish green or brown in colour and up to 47mm (1¾in) long. Two or three generations occur between spring and autumn. The caterpillars often bore into the heads of cabbages where they soil the edible part with their excrement. Control newly hatched caterpillars with pyrethrum or bifenthrin, but not those feeding inside the heads.

Cabbage root fly

The white maggots are up to 8mm (⅜in) long. They eat the roots of leafy brassicas, often killing young transplants. They also tunnel into the roots of turnip, swedes, and radish. There are no insecticides available for this pest. Place brassica collars around the stem bases of transplants to deter egg laying, or grow susceptible plants under horticultural fleece.

Cabbage white butterflies

Damage is caused by the pale green velvety caterpillars of the small cabbage white and the yellow and black hairy caterpillars of the large cabbage white. The latter feed on the outer leaves and small white caterpillars bore into cabbage heads. Prevent butterflies from laying eggs by growing under fine mesh netting. For caterpillar control, see cabbage moth (*above*).

Cabbage whitefly

The adults are white-winged insects about 2mm (¹⁄₁₂in) in length. Both the adults and their flat, oval, scale-like nymphs suck sap from the underside of the leaves. This pest attacks all leafy brassicas and is active all year round. Heavy infestations soil the foliage with honeydew and sooty mould. Spray with pyrethrum, plant oils, fatty acids, or bifenthrin.

Mealy cabbage aphid

Dense colonies of whitish grey aphids develop on the underside of brassica leaves during the summer. The leaves become yellowish white above where the aphids are feeding. The growing points of young cabbages may be killed, causing "blind" plants. Spray with pyrethrum, plant oils, fatty acids, or bifenthrin, particularly if aphids are seen on young plants.

Potatoes and parsnips

Parsnips and potatoes are not difficult to grow, but it can be difficult to grow them to perfection because of the pests and diseases that affect them.

If you have damage on:
- Turnips and swedes, see brassica flea beetles (*p.114*) and cabbage root fly (*p.115*)

See also:
- General pests and diseases on vegetables (*pp.108–109*)
- Know your enemy: pests and diseases (*pp.26–43*)
- Carrot fly (*p.121*)
- Crop rotation (*p.23*)
- Barriers and repellents (*pp.58–59*)

Potato cyst eelworm
The nematodes develop inside the roots, causing the foliage to die from the bottom of the plant up. Early death of the plants results in a poor crop of small tubers. Mature nematodes appear as brown pinhead-sized objects attached to the roots. Each contains hundreds of eggs. There is no chemical treatment. Grow resistant potato cultivars on a long rotation.

Potato early blight
Dark brown spots with concentric rings surrounded by a chlorotic halo appear on the leaves, which may become necrotic and remain attached. Tuber lesions develop a dry rot. Warm wet conditions favour development. Remove debris, rotate crops, and use healthy seeds. Applying fertilizers and adequate water make the crop less susceptible.

Potato common scab
Scabby spots develop on the skin with irregular edges when the skin ruptures. The tubers are unsightly, but the damage is not serious. It occurs on light soils that lack organic matter and is worst in dry years. Dig in organic matter and water regularly when the tubers form. Do not grow on ground limed for a previous brassica crop. Resistant varieties are available.

Potato blackleg
This is a bacterial disease that can be present in seed tubers. Only one or two stems may be affected and these blacken and rot at ground level. Remove affected plants to avoid infection of tubers as these would not keep well. The disease is encouraged by wet soil, but potato blackleg does not persist in the soil. Buy good quality seed tubers.

Potato dry rot
Tuber infection by dry rot *Fusarium* species only occurs through wounds. Sunken lesions with concentric rings and a white fungus can appear. Tubers become mummified. Infected seed tubers may fail to emerge or produce poor growth. Ensure they are mature when harvested and stored in a cool, well ventilated place. Cultivars vary in their susceptibility.

Potato blight

Dead patches at the tip of the leaflets enlarge to kill the leaf. The infection spreads rapidly under wet conditions with spores washed to the ground to infect the tubers. The rot is a hard, reddish-brown patch. Affected tubers will not store. Airborne spores can infect plants even when no diseased material is present. Spray foliage with a fungicide before the blight appears.

Potato gangrene

This fungus causes depressions on the tuber surface. When cut across the lesion, a dark rot extends into the flesh. Black fungal structures may be in the lesion cavities and on the surface. Infected tubers are usually the source of gangrene, which invades through wounding, so try not to damage during harvesting. Destroy infected tubers.

Potato silver scurf

This is a storage disease where the fungus causes roughly circular, silver lesions on the skin that usually enlarge during storage. It does not cause yield loss but affects vigour. Transmission is through infected seeds or spores in the soil. There is no effective control, so to avoid the incidence, delay harvesting, dry rapidly, and store hygienically.

Potato spraing

Spraing symptoms are dark line and rings on the surface, and arcs, lines, or brown flecks are visible in the flesh. Plants may be stunted, leaves yellowed or mottled, and tubers malformed. Destroy infected plants, plant healthy tubers, control weeds (as they can carry viruses), rotate crops, and avoid high level of irrigation at tuber initiation.

Parsnip canker

The fungi that cause this canker occur where lesions develop on the root. They also cause leaf spots from which spores are washed down to the soil to infect the roots through wounds. The fungi can be transmitted on or in the seed. They survive in crop debris, so remove. Rotate crops and use resistant cultivars. Earthing up may prevent the spores reaching the roots.

Parsnip viruses

Yellow fleck virus causes bold yellow veins and vein netting, and then yellow flecks and mosaics. It is transmitted by several species of aphids. A helper virus is required for transmission. Weeds act as virus reservoirs as they are susceptible to both viruses. Parsnip, carrot, and celery are immune to the helper virus. Avoid susceptible hosts, control weed hosts, and spray the aphids.

Salad crops

Most salads, like lettuces, are easy to grow; others, like tomatoes, might need a bit of experience to avoid common problems.

If you have damage on:
- Radishes, see brassica flea beetles (*p.114*), brassica downy mildew (*p.114*), and cabbage root fly (*p.115*)

See also:
- General pests and diseases on vegetables (*pp.108–109*)
- Know your enemy: pests and diseases (*pp.26–43*)
- Calcium and potassium deficiency effects on tomatoes (*p.15*)
- Crop rotation (*p.23*)
- Barriers and repellents (*pp.58–59*)
- Glasshouse pests (*pp.134–139*)

Lettuce root aphid

The brownish white aphids suck sap from the roots of lettuce during the summer, causing slow growth and wilting in dry weather. They secrete a white waxy powder that coats the roots and nearby soil particles. There is no effective insecticide available for this pest. Some lettuce cultivars, such as 'Avoncrisp', 'Lakeland', and 'Sigmaball', are resistant to the aphid.

Lettuce downy mildew

Pale green or yellow areas develop on the upper surface of the leaves and eventually tissues die. Whitish mould develops beneath the affected areas. The disease spreads mainly by air-borne spores, but the fungus can also survive in the soil. Dispose of affected plants, maintain a long rotation between lettuce crops, and use resistant cultivars or the fungicide mancozeb.

Lettuce viruses

Various viruses can affect lettuce including beet western yellow virus, lettuce mosaic virus, lettuce big vein virus, and tomato spotted wilt virus. Symptoms of any of these viruses include vein clearing, yellowing, mosaic patterning, and deformation. Plants may be stunted. Use tolerant cultivars, remove weed hosts, and control aphids with insecticide.

Tomato moth

The caterpillars of tomato moths are brown or pale green with a thin yellow line along the sides. They are up to 40mm (1½in) long and between mid- and late summer they eat the foliage and fruits of tomatoes. When fully fed, the caterpillars go into the soil to pupate. Remove the caterpillars by hand or spray with pyrethrum or bifenthrin.

Tomato ghost spot

Ghost spot is a distinct symptom of white or yellow rings on tomatoes that occur when the fungus *Botrytis cinerea* invades the tomato fruit, but it dies prior to causing decay. The fruits develop normally and are still edible, so there is no need to dispose of them. To help remove spread of infection, reduce plant wetness and improve ventilation.

Tomato leaf mould

Patches of grey mould grow on leaf undersides and soon develop on the upper sides and turn yellow. The disease is encouraged by warm and humid conditions. The fungus survives on plant debris and greenhouse structures during winter. Good ventilation helps to prevent the disease. Resistant varieties are available. Copper fungicides give incidental control.

Tomato viruses

Typically, viruses on tomatoes cause mottling and distortion of leaves, stunting, and poor fruit yield. However, it should be noted that some symptoms are very similar to those caused by herbicide exposure or cold damage. Of those that affect tomatoes, tomato mosaic virus (TMV) is a highly contagious and serious virus. Fruit can fail to set and young fruit is "bronzed" or streaked. If symptoms are seen, destroy plants immediately, although extensive spread may have occurred but not yet be obvious. Tools and hands should be cleaned well. Pest control is important. Some cultivars are marketed as resistant to TMV. Cucumber mosaic virus can also affect tomatoes (*see below*).

Tomato blight

Outdoor tomato plants are particularly at risk of blight and symptoms are similar to those on potato (*see p.117*). Infected fruit discolours and they rot rapidly. If fruit is picked from diseased plants, keep for five days to see if any rot develops. If nothing happens, it is safe to eat. Spray plants as soon as the first truss has set and then at ten-day intervals.

Cucumber powdery mildew

Several powdery mildew species infect cucurbits, causing early ageing and reduction in yields. A white powdery growth appears on the leaves, petioles, and stems. Fruits are rarely affected. It is air-borne and survives the winter on their hosts, including weeds. Improve ventilation, and use resistant cultivars. Sulphur can be used as a control on edible plants.

Cucumber mosaic virus (CMV)

This is one of the most common plant viruses, causing yellow mottling, distorted leaves, stunted growth, and a range of other symptoms on a wide range of plants. CMV is aphid and mechanically transmitted. Destroy infected plants, practise aphid control, remove weeds, and minimize handling. Sterilize tools and wash hands. Grow resistant varieties.

Assorted vegetables

Vegetable growers need to be aware of the most common problems.

If you have damage on:
- Beetroot and Swiss chard, see beet leaf miner (*opposite*)
- Celeriac, see celery leaf miner and celery leaf spot (*opposite*)
- Parsley, parsnips, celery, and cereriac, see carrot fly (*opposite*)
- Radishes, see brassica flea beetles (*p.114*), brassica downy mildew (*p.114*), and cabbage root fly (*p.115*)
- Turnips and swedes, see brassica flea beetles (*p.114*) and cabbage root fly (*p.115*)

See also:
- General pests and diseases on vegetables (*pp.108–109*)
- Know your enemy: pests and diseases (*pp.26–43*)

Allium leaf miner
This small fly lays eggs on leeks, onions, and related plants. The white maggots feed as leaf miners and bore into leek stems. The brown pupal stage is often found beneath the base of leek leaves. Currently a problem in the Midlands, but it will spread. No effective insecticide is available so protect plants by growing them under horticultural fleece.

Leek moth
The whitish green caterpillars are up to 11mm (½in) long. They live as leaf miners and also tunnel into the stems and bulbs of leeks and onions. There are two generations in early and late summer. Small plants develop secondary rots and may be killed. There is no effective insecticide available. Protect plants by growing them under horticultural fleece.

Leek white tip
The cause of white tip is the soil-borne fungus-like *Phytophthora porri*. It is specific to alliums. It causes watersoaked, elliptical blotches, mostly at tips of leaves. Badly affected leaves rot and plants may be stunted or killed. On onions and garlic, it also causes root rot. Rotate susceptible alliums with at least a three-year gap with non-host crops.

Onion fly
The white maggots are up to 9mm (³⁄₈in) long and there can be three generations between late spring and early autumn. They eat the roots and bore into the base of onions, leeks, and allied vegetables. Young plants are often killed. There is no effective insecticide available. Plants can be protected by growing them under horticultural fleece.

Onion white rot
White fluffy growth appears on roots and basal tissues, which rot, sometimes causing plants to fall over. Leaves yellow and die. Destroy affected plants. The fungus produces black resting spores that can survive in the soil for 15 years, so take care not to spread contaminated soil. Grow allium species on a different site or replace affected soil.

Onion neck rot

This disease is seedborne and mainly found in storage. Softening and browning of the scales is then covered by a dense grey mould. Eventually, the bulbs suffer from dry rot and become mummified. The fungus forms sclerotia, which survive in the soil. A four-year crop rotation is recommended. Ensure the plants are dry before storing in a cool dry place.

Asparagus beetle

Both the adult beetles and their creamy black grubs eat the foliage and gnaw the bark off the stems. The beetles are black with yellow and red markings and are 6–7mm (¼in) long. The grubs are up to 8mm (⅜in) long. Asparagus plants that are heavily infested become defoliated and the stems die prematurely. Remove the pest by hand or spray with pyrethrum.

Carrot fly

Carrots, parsnips, and parsley roots are tunnelled by slender, pale yellow larvae that are up to 10mm (½in) long. Three generations can occur between early summer and the autumn. No effective insecticide is available so protect plants by growing them under horticultural fleece. Some carrot cultivars, 'Fly-Away', 'Maestro', and 'Resistafly' are less susceptible.

Beet leaf miner

The leaves of beetroot, Swiss chard, and spinach beet are mined by the maggots of this fly. The affected areas of the leaves turn white or pale green, then go brown and dry up. Two generations occur in early and late summer. This pest is difficult to control with insecticides, so pick off infested leaves or grow the plants under horticultural fleece.

Celery leaf miner

Maggots of this small fly mine the leaves of celery, celeriac, and lovage, causing brown, dried-up blotches in the foliage. Two generations occur in early and late summer. Damage to young plants slows growth and makes celery stems stringy. This pest is difficult to control with insecticides, so pick off infested leaves or grow the plants under horticultural fleece.

Celery leaf spot

This seed-borne disease affects celery and celeriac. Small chlorotic, angular spots that turn brown contain the black fruiting bodies of the fungus. As the disease progresses, entire leaves become blighted. Severe infections are associated with long periods of rain. Destroy infected plant debris, use disease free seeds, rotate crops, and avoid overhead irrigation.

Fruit trees: apples and pears

Fruit trees have many pests and diseases that damage the fruits, foliage, and branches.

See also:
- General pests and diseases on fruit (*pp.110–111*) and trees, shrubs, and climbers (*pp.66–69*)
- Know your enemy: pests and diseases (*pp.26–43*)
- Crown gall (*p.68*)
- Mice and rats (*p.36*)
- Powdery mildew (*p.40*)
- Scabs (*p.41*)
- Tortrix moth (*pp.90 and 138*)
- The effects of calcium and potassium deficiencies (*p.15*)
- Traps (*pp.56–57*)
- Barriers and repellents (*pp.58–59*)

Apple sawfly
The caterpillar-like larvae feed inside apples at the fruitlet stage. Damaged fruitlets usually fall in early summer. Those that stay on the tree develop a long, broad, brownish yellow scar on the fruit skin by late summer. Remove damaged fruitlets when seen. If the tree was heavily attacked last year, spray with bifenthrin at petal fall to control the hatching larvae.

Apple capsid
This bug sucks sap from the shoot tips, causing the leaves to tear into many small holes. More noticeable, however, is the damage caused by feeding on the young fruitlets. These mature as ripe fruits that have raised corky bumps. The blemishes do not affect the eating or keeping qualities, so it is a pest that can be tolerated on garden trees.

Apple codling moth
The caterpillars feed in the cores of ripening apple and sometimes pear fruits. By the time the fruit is ready for picking, the caterpillar has usually left through an exit tunnel. Codling moth pheromone traps can be used in early summer to time sprays of bifenthrin more accurately to control the recently hatched caterpillars before they enter the fruits.

Apple leaf mining moth
The tiny caterpillars feed inside the leaves of apples and cherries, creating long, narrow, twisting white or brown lines on the upper leaf surface. Several generations occur during the summer but heavy infestations are generally not seen before late summer. By then, it is too late for the pest to damage the tree, so control measures are not required.

Rosy apple aphid
In spring, rosy apple aphids suck sap from the young foliage and developing fruitlets. This causes yellowing and curled leaves at the shoot tips. Affected fruits fail to grow to full size and have a pinched appearance at the eye end. Spray the newly hatched greyish pink aphids with plant oils, bifenthrin, or thiacloprid just before the flower buds open.

Apple and pear canker

This canker grows near buds or wounds, which become elliptical with concentric rings of shrunken bark. Spores enter through wounds. Prune out small cankered branches; on larger limbs, chisel back to green wood and treat wounds with wound paint. Spray in autumn with a copper fungicide after harvest and again after half the leaves have fallen.

Pear and cherry slugworm

The larvae of this sawfly are up to 9mm (³⁄₈in) long and covered in black slime. They graze away the leaf surface, creating brown dried-up areas. Pear, cherries, plums, *Sorbus*, *Chaenomeles*, and hawthorn are attacked by two or three generations between summer and autumn. If numerous, control by spraying with pyrethrum or bifenthrin.

Pear bedstraw aphid

Dense infestations of this grey aphid can occur on pears in spring and early summer. It then migrates to wild flowers known as bedstraws for the rest of the summer. Pear foliage becomes yellowish and distorted; it is also sticky with honeydew excreted by the aphids. Control by spraying with bifenthrin, thiacloprid, or plant oils after flowering.

Pear fruitlet midge

This gall midge lays eggs on unopened pear flower buds. Orange white maggots, up to 3mm (⅛in) long, feed inside the fruitlets. These turn black, starting at the eye end, and drop off in early summer. Destroy infested fruitlets before the maggots complete their feeding. Spray small trees with bifenthrin at the white bud stage to control the adult flies.

Pear rust

Bright orange blotches appear on pear leaves in summer. Fruit and twigs are occasionally infected. The fungus alternates on juniper, causing perennial swelling on branches that release spores in spring. Removal of affected junipers may solve pear infection, but spores can still be blown some distance. Treating trees for scab will give incidental control.

Pear brown rot

Many fruit trees can be affected by this fungal disease. Spots of soft brown rot develop on fruit and rapidly enlarge. Rings of buff spores appear on this tissue and will initiate more infections. Rotten fruit becomes mummified and remains on the tree. The fungus can grow back into the spur. Prune out diseased spurs and remove all rotten fruit from the tree.

Fruit trees: *Prunus*

Cherries, plums, apricots, nectarines, and peaches all belong to the same group of stone fruit and suffer similar problems.

See also:
- General pests and diseases on fruit (*pp.110–111*) and trees, shrubs, and climbers (*pp.66–69*)
- Know your enemy: pests and diseases (*pp.26–43*)
- Crown gall (*p.68*)
- Hydrangea scale (*p.80*)
- Pear and cherry slugworm (*p.123*)
- Pear brown rot (*p.123*)
- Silver leaf (*see p.43*)
- Water lily aphid (*p.93*)
- Wisteria scale (*p.85*)
- Witches' broom (*p.68*)
- Traps (*pp.56–57*)
- Barriers and repellents (*pp.58–59*)

Bacterial canker
Lesions appear on branches and tissue dies above this point. Gum exudation may occur from the canker. In late autumn, bacteria from the leaves are splashed on to the bark to produce new cankers. Pruning during active growth and spraying trees with Bordeaux mixture in autumn helps prevent bark infection. Some plum and cherry cultivars show resistance.

Peach leaf curl
Peach leaf curl affects peaches, nectarines, and close relatives. Red or pale green blisters develop on new leaves, which swell and curl, and are later covered in white spores. Some of which overwinter on dormant shoots. Apply a copper fungicide as buds begin to swell in late January and a fortnight later. Spray before leaf fall and remove diseased tissue.

Cherry blackfly
Black aphids infest the shoot tips of fruiting and some ornamental cherries (not Japanese cherries). The leaves are curled and distorted, sticky with honeydew, and may turn brown. Infestations die out in midsummer. On trees small enough to spray, watch for blackfly in spring and spray with thiacloprid, pyrethrum, or plant oils before extensive leaf curling occurs.

Cherry leaf scorch
A leaf-killing disease of *Prunus avium* causes brown blotches to develop on the leaves during summer, which die but don't fall, even during winter. Normal growth will resume in spring. No adverse effects on the tree are seen and control is not necessary, although it may be worth removing infected leaves as they occur. Do not compost them.

Cherry leaf spot
This fungus *Blumeriella jaapii* causes round purplish spots later turning brown on *Prunus* species. Eventually the dead tissues fall out to leave shot holes. Premature defoliation occurs and a white fungus may be seen under the leaf surfaces. Destroy infected leaves. A copper fungicide to control bacterial canker should give some incidental control.

Mealy plum aphid

Dense colonies of whitish green aphids develop in midsummer on plum leaves and shoot tips. Large amounts of honeydew are excreted and sooty moulds grow on the foliage and fruits. Spray small trees with thiacloprid, pyrethrum, or plant oils as soon as this pest is spotted. Sooty mould and honeydew can be wiped off fruits with a damp cloth.

Plum gall mite

Whitish green swellings develop on the foliage of plums and damsons, especially around the margins, from late spring onwards. They are induced by microscopic mites that live and feed inside the galls. Apart from creating the galls, the mites have no adverse effect on the tree or fruits, which is fortunate as there is no effective chemical control.

Plum leaf-curling aphid

This greenfly hatches in early spring from overwintered eggs. It sucks sap from emerging leaves, causing crinkled and curled leaves on plum and damson. Infestations end in early summer but damaged foliage remains distorted. Apply a winter plant oil spray in midwinter to kill the eggs. Spray small trees at bud burst with a ready-to-use thiacloprid formulation.

Plum moth

Small pink caterpillars feed inside the fruits of plums, damsons, and greengages in late summer. Damaged fruits tend to ripen early, so later ripening fruits are less likely to be maggoty. This is difficult to control as effective insecticides are not available to gardeners. Plum moth pheromone traps can be used in early summer to capture male plum moths.

Plum sawfly

This pest has caterpillar-like larvae that bore into plums at the fruitlet stage in spring. Damaged fruitlets usually fail to develop and then drop off in early summer. There are no effective chemical controls available to gardeners for plum sawfly. In years when there has been an average to good set of fruits, the loss of some fruitlets can be tolerated.

Pocket plum

Fruits are twisted, usually one-sided, and often banana shaped. Their skin is pale green and smooth and there is no stone. A white spore develops over the surface and the plums shrivel. The fungus can overwinter in twigs. There is no chemical control so remove affected plums. This disease rarely affects all the fruits and may not reappear for several years.

Soft fruit

Perishable berries like currants, gooseberries, grapes, and mulberries are dealt with here. More often than not, it is the leaves, buds, and stems that are affected.

If you have damage on:
- Gooseberries, see also currant leaf spot (*below*)
- Redcurrant, see also gooseberry sawflies (*opposite*)

See also:
- General pests and diseases on fruit (*pp.110–111*)
- Know your enemy: pests and diseases (*pp.26–43*)
- Coral spot (*p.67*)

Blackcurrant gall midge
This tiny fly lays eggs on emerging leaves at the shoot tips. There are at least three generations during late spring and summer. The white maggots, up to 3mm (⅛in) long, prevent the normal expansion of the leaves, which remain small and distorted. There are no insecticide controls for garden use so the leaf damage has to be tolerated.

Currant blister aphid
In spring–early summer, leaves at the shoot tips of red- and blackcurrants become puckered with a red or yellowish green discolouration. Pale yellow aphids suck sap from beneath the leaves. Infestations die out in midsummer. Use a plant oil winter wash to control the overwintering eggs. After bud burst, use thiacloprid or pyrethrum to deal with the aphids.

Currant leaf spot
A fungus causes spots or blotches on the leaves from May onwards. The spots appear first on the older leaves, which may turn yellow if the spots are numerous. The disease causes the leaves to fall prematurely. Spots can occur on stems, leaf stalks, and on unripe fruits, which shrivel. Dispose of fallen material to reduce the risk of infection for the following year.

Blackcurrant big bud mite
Microscopic mites live inside blackcurrant buds, making them abnormally swollen and rounded over the winter. Galled buds fail to develop and dry up, which reduces the plant's cropping potential. There are no chemical controls so pick off infested buds in winter or replace heavily infested unproductive plants. The cultivar 'Ben Hope' is resistant.

Gooseberry sawflies

Several species of sawfly larvae feed on the foliage of gooseberry and redcurrant, sometimes causing complete defoliation. The caterpillar-like larvae are up to 20mm (¾in) long and pale green, often marked with black dots. Two or three generations occur between spring and the end of summer. Search for the larvae and spray with pyrethrum or thiacloprid.

American gooseberry mildew

Powdery white patches develop on leaves and young shoots, causing leaves to die and shoots to be stunted. Gooseberry fruits are also badly affected. Prune infected tissue to encourage good airflow, and use a fungicide, but avoid excessive use of nitrogenous fertilizers. Keep watered and mulched in dry periods. Resistant varieties are available.

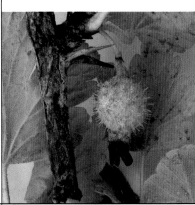

Grape erinose mite

Grape vine leaves develop a puckered appearance with a dense coating of creamy white or sometimes pink hairs underneath the raised areas. This abnormal growth is induced by microscopic gall mites. Apart from causing the leaf distortion, the mite has no harmful effect on the vine's growth or fruit. It has to be tolerated as there is no effective control.

Mulberry blight

Water-soaked spots that coalesce, turning brown and sometimes surrounded by a yellow halo, are seen on the leaves. These become distorted. Young shoots may die back from which bacterial slime oozes. The bacterium can survive in leaf debris in the soil. Use healthy planting material, avoid overhead irrigation, and remove dead shoots to manage the disease.

Mulberry leaf spot

Mycosphaerella mori is a common leaf spot fungus on mulberry. It causes dark spots, which become larger and paler as the infection progresses. The spores of the fungus are water splashed, so the infection is more commonly seen during wet summers. It can cause serious defoliation. Remove infected leaves to reduce the spread of the disease.

Red berry mite

This microscopic mite attacks blackberry fruits and interferes with the ripening process, causing fruits to remain partly or wholly red. This pest is more troublesome in hot summers. The first fruits usually ripen properly but incomplete ripening increases in the following weeks. There is no effective treatment. Use partly ripe fruit for cooking or jam making.

Raspberries and strawberries

Expensive in the shops, it makes sense to grow your own berries. Moulds are a problem, but watch out for other troubles.

If you have damage on:
- Blackberries, see raspberry spur blight (*below*)

See also:
- General pests and diseases on fruit (*pp.110–111*)
- Know your enemy: pests and diseases (*pp.26–43*)
- Crown gall (*p.68*)
- Barriers and repellents (*pp.58–59*)

If millipedes (*see p.34*) are a problem on strawberries, protect the fruit by lifting them clear from the soil with a bed of straw.

Raspberry beetle
The slender brownish white grubs, up to 8mm (³⁄₈in) long, feed on the berries of raspberry and other cane fruits. They feed at the stalk end of the berry, causing dried-up patches. This is a difficult pest to control. Spraying with pyrethrum when the first pink fruits appear, with a second application two weeks later, will give some control.

Raspberry leaf and bud mite
The microscopic mites live on the underside of the leaves where they suck sap. This causes pale yellow blotches on the upper leaf surface that can be mistaken for a virus infection. Mite-infested canes grow to the usual height and produce a reasonable crop of fruit, unlike virus-infected plants. There is no control for the mite.

Raspberry spur blight
Small, elliptical purple spots appear around the buds on raspberry and loganberry canes in early summer. They enlarge over the autumn. The infection kills many buds making canes unfruitful. It overwinters on canes, so remove affected tissue. Don't overfeed with nitrogen and thin overcrowded plants. Copper oxychloride may give some protection.

Raspberry cane blight
In summer, raspberry canes may suddenly die back. At the stem base a brown lesion is present, the bark ruptures, and the stem is brittle. The causal fungus infects through wounds, so minimize damage by pruning and training. Cut back diseased wood to healthy tissue. Avoid waterlogged conditions and encourage good airflow between canes.

Raspberry powdery mildew
Several species affect raspberries. A whitish powdery coat covers foliage, canes, and fruits. Pale green blotches appear on the upper surface of the leaves. Severe infection affects growth. Infected fruit may be covered with a white fungus. Severely infected berries fail to develop. Practise good hygiene and improve ventilation. Sulphur can control mildew on edible plants.

Raspberry rust

Yellow pustules appear on the upper leaf surfaces of raspberries in early summer. Later, orange then black pustules develop on the lower surfaces and defoliation may subsequently result. To control the rust, destroy infected material, spray the plants with a copper oxychloride before the fruit ripen, and choose less susceptible varieties.

Strawberry seed beetle

Several species of black beetles, about 15mm (⅝in) long, damage strawberry fruits by eating the seeds on the outside of the berry. This causes brown discolouration and may encourage rotting. Strawberry seed beetles also feed on weed seeds, so keep the strawberry bed weed free to discourage them. There is no suitable insecticide treatment.

Strawberry green petal

Green petal is a leafhopper-borne disease. Flowers are reduced and have green petals. Cropping is poor and fruits are deformed. The plant is stunted and leaves turn red after flowering. Destroy affected plants and spray against leafhoppers. Always use certified stock when planting and replace the plants every two or three years.

Strawberry grey mould

The fungus *Botrytis cinerea* enters through the flowers and remains dormant until the fruits mature, where it can be seen as greyish growth. It spreads by contact or air-borne spores and survives on plant debris or in the soil as sclerotia. Remove infected parts and plant debris. Apply a light straw covering around plants and remove weeds.

Strawberry leaf spot

White spots on strawberry leaves surrounded by a purple border are caused by the fungus *Mycosphaerella fragariae*. Lesions occur on flowers, fruits, and stems. Its effect on plant growth is not severe. The fungus is spread by rain splash. To control the leaf spot, remove plant debris on which the fungus overwinters and use resistant cultivars.

Strawberry viruses

Many viruses can cause decline of strawberries. Symptoms vary depending on the viruses, cultivar, and environment, but include plant stunting, yellowing, and distortion and discolouration of the leaves. Destroy infected plants and control the vector if the virus is known. Use certified virus-free stocks and resistant cultivars.

Herbs

Many herbs are trouble-free, but there are a couple of quite serious pests and diseases to consider on some of the most common species, such as rosemary beetle.

If you have damage on:
- Sage and thyme, see rosemary beetle (*right*)
- Marjoram and savory, see mint rust (*opposite*)

See also:
- Know your enemy: pests and diseases (*pp.26–43*)

Rosemary beetle
The foliage of rosemary, lavender, thyme, and sage is eaten by the beetles and their greyish white grubs. The damage occurs from late summer until the following spring. The adult beetles are 7–8mm (¼–⅜in) long and have purple and green stripes on their wing cases. Collect the adults and larvae by shaking the plant over a sheet of newspaper, or spray with thiacloprid.

Sage leafhopper
The mottled yellow and grey insects are up to 3mm (⅛in) long and readily jump off herb plants when disturbed. They suck sap and cause a coarse pale mottling of the upper leaf surface. This seems to have little impact on the plants' flavour or vigour so the pest can be tolerated. If required, the plants could be sprayed with pyrethrum or thiacloprid.

Bay sucker
The leaf margin, usually on one side of a leaf, becomes yellowish, thickened and curled over. This is caused by bay sucker nymphs, which are sucking sap from underneath the curled leaf margin. Later, the damaged part of the leaf dries up and turns brown. Two generations of this insect occur during the summer. When the nymphs are ready to moult to the adult stage, they emerge from beneath the leaves as grey, flattened insects that secrete white waxy fibres from their bodies. Adult bay suckers may be seen on the shoot tips in summer. They resemble aphids, have wings, and are 2mm (¹⁄₁₂in) long. Pick off infested leaves as they develop or spray with thiacloprid when the leaf curling begins.

Bay powdery mildew
Whitish patches develop on the surfaces of the leaves, which become distorted in spring and summer. Dark necrotic spots then develop as a result of infection and infected leaves may fall. Increasing ventilation and making sure the roots do not get dry help to prevent the disease. Spray the plant with sulphur if the leaves are used for cooking.

Mint rust

Affected stems and leaves are pale and distorted before masses of orange pustules erupt on affected areas of the stem and the lower leaf surface. These turn black as the infection develops. Leaf tissue dies and plants are defoliated. The fungus *Puccinia menthae* is perennial in garden mint and related plants, such as marjoram and savory, but spores also overwinter in the soil to infect new shoots the following spring. Use of a flame gun to remove debris in the autumn and kill spores on the soil can be effective. If healthy plants cannot be obtained, heat treatment of mint rhizomes at exactly 44°C (111°F) for ten minutes before swirling them in cold water and planting is used commercially.

Lavender grey mould

Die-back of lavender can be caused by several pathogens. Some fungi enter through wounds and can be seen as black fruiting bodies (lavender shab) or grey fluffy mould (*Botrytis*) on the dead stems. *Phytophthora* causes a root rot and the plant then dies. Except for *Phytophthora* root rot, the diseases may be controlled by cutting out the infected stems.

Mint beetle

The adult beetles are a shiny emerald green colour and are about 10mm (½in) long. Both the beetles and their matte black grubs eat the foliage of mints during late spring and summer. The beetle is rarely so abundant that it causes serious damage. Remove it by hand – its bright colouring makes it is easy to see – rather than unnecessarily using a pesticide.

Cuckoo spit

Lavender is particularly attractive to sap-sucking insects called froghoppers, but they also occur on other herbs and garden flowers. The immature nymphs feed from the stems in late spring to early summer and surround themselves with a white frothy liquid called cuckoo spit. Little harm is done to the plant, so insecticide treatment is not required.

Glasshouses

The warm protected environment of a greenhouse allows gardeners to grow tender plants. It also provides ideal conditions for certain pests to reproduce rapidly and develop damaging infestations, which if not dealt with promptly, can overwhelm the plants. Enclosed structures, such as greenhouses and conservatories, are ideal for the use of biological controls during the summer months. Under suitable conditions, these predators and parasites are effective in keeping the main glasshouse pests at a low level without the use of pesticides. Glasshouse diseases are less troublesome, but need watching out for nevertheless.

Pests and diseases under cover

Plants grown in greenhouses, polythene tunnels, or as house plants enjoy warm, sheltered conditions that also favour certain pests. The abundance of soft growth and high temperatures allows pests to breed rapidly. Diseases can be less troublesome under cover but some, such as grey mould, thrive in high humidity.

Treatments and controls

Pesticides can control pests and diseases but are not suitable for all plants and have restricted uses on edible plants. Another problem is that pests that reproduce rapidly have numerous generations each year and quickly gain resistance to chemical controls. For many greenhouse pests there are alternative biological controls using natural enemies to keep pests at a low level. This avoids resistance problems and can be used on all types of plants. The predators, parasites, or pathogenic nematodes are supplied by mail order biocontrol suppliers or can be ordered through garden centres. Predators and parasites are susceptible to synthetic pesticides, so biological control is an alternative, rather than something to be tried after spraying has failed. Introduce natural enemies before heavy infestations have developed. They require relatively warm daytime temperatures and good light intensity, so cannot be used in winter. If a heavy infestation is present before it is time to introduce the biological control, spray with a short persistence organic pesticide, such as fatty acids or plant oils.

The mealybug ladybird (*Cryptolaemus montrouzieri*) and its larvae eat mealybugs and their eggs.

A predatory mite (*Phytoseiulus persimilis*) attacks a glasshouse red spider mite and its eggs.

A pathogenic nematode (*Phasmarhabditis hermaphrodita*) infects slugs with a fatal disease.

A parasitic wasp (*Encarsia formosa*) develops in glasshouse whitefly nymphs and kills them.

Remove dead flowers and leaves and provide space between plants to reduce fungal infections.

Integrated controls

Integrated control applies to greenhouse problems just as much as to garden pests and diseases. It involves the use of various compatible control measures instead of relying on a single control strategy, such as spraying with pesticides. This includes good cultivation practices, the use of pest- or disease-resistant plants, barriers to exclude pests, sticky traps, and encouraging natural enemies or augmenting them with bought-in biological controls. Pesticides also have a role, but try to select those with a short persistence, especially if biocontrols are going to be used.

Good hygiene is important for preventing the development of diseases in greenhouses. Grey mould (*see p.136*) often develops on dead flowers or yellowing leaves and spreads from there to live tissues, so inspect plants regularly and pick off such material. Grey mould and other diseases, such as pelargonium rust (*see p.94*), thrive where plants are overcrowded and growing in humid conditions. Try to give plants space, prune out dense growth, and keep the greenhouse ventilated. Keeping the greenhouse tidy will also remove hiding places for slugs and other pests. Plants that have become badly affected by pests or diseases are best removed as they may not recover and the problem is likely to spread to other plants.

Greenhouses can get excessively hot in the summer and opening doors and ventilators may not be sufficient to keep the temperature down. Fitting roller blinds or painting the glass with a shading material will help. In early autumn, remove the shading as plants will need full light over the winter months.

Greenhouses need plenty of ventilation on sunny days to prevent plants overheating.

Use a max-min thermometer to record temperatures.

Make sure plants have a regular supply of water.

Glasshouse pests and diseases

Anyone who owns a glasshouse will be familiar with the common problems, such as whitefly and grey mould, but be vigilant for other, less visible, disorders.

If you have damage on:
- Begonias, see vine weevil grub (*p.138*) and glasshouse viruses (*p.139*)
- Cyclamen, see vine weevil grub (*p.138*)
- Tomatoes, see tomato leaf mould (*p.119*) and glasshouse viruses (*p.139*)
- See also chrysanthemum leaf miner (*p.95*), and leaf and bud eelworms (*p.91*)

Glasshouse red spider mite
Large numbers of barely visible yellowish green mites live under the foliage on many glasshouse plants. They cause a fine pale mottling of the upper leaf surface, with leaves yellowing and dropping. A fine silk webbing can be seen in heavy infestations. Use a predatory mite, *Phytoseiulus*, for biocontrol, or spray with bifenthrin, plant oils, or fatty acids.

Grey mould
Affected plant tissue rots and becomes covered in grey fluffy mould (*Botrytis cinerea*). Flowers may develop small brown spots on the petals. As it can spread very rapidly by contact between diseased and healthy tissue, ensure that dead plant material is promptly removed. This helps reduce grey mould parasitizing healthy plants. Keeping the glasshouse ventilated and watering in the morning will reduce humid conditions, which encourage the fungus. Grey mould can be a problem on grapes under glass, often infecting through the scar tissue produced by powdery mildew infection. Trying to limit powdery mildew infection should reduce the grey mould damage.

Glasshouse whitefly
The white-winged adults and their whitish green nymphs are up to 2mm (¹⁄₁₂in) long. They suck sap from the leaf undersides of tomato, cucumber, and many ornamental plants. They excrete honeydew on which sooty mould grows. Use a parasitic wasp, *Encarsia*, as a biocontrol, or spray with thiacloprid, acetamiprid, bifenthrin, pyrethrum, plant oils, or fatty acids.

Fluted scale

This sap-sucking insect occurs on many plants, especially citrus plants and *Acacia* species. The mature females deposit their eggs in white waxy mounds that look grooved or fluted. Heavy infestations weaken plants and soil them with honeydew. Spray with thiacloprid, acetamiprid, or plant oils. On small plants, pick off the scales and their eggs.

Hemispherical scale

The mature females are covered by brown hemispherical shells or scales that are 2–4mm (1/12–1/8in) in diameter. It infests the leaves and stems of many ornamental plants in heated greenhouses, making them sticky with honeydew. Spray affected plants with thiacloprid, acetamiprid, fatty acids, or plant oils. On small plants, wipe them off with a damp cloth.

Oleander scale

This sap-sucking insect infests the leaves and stems of many ornamental plants in greenhouses. The mature insects are covered by flat circular scales, 2mm (1/12in) in diameter, that are whitish grey with a yellowish brown centre. No honeydew is produced but heavily infested plants are weakened. Spray with thiacloprid, acetamiprid, fatty acids, or plant oils.

Soft scale

Soft scale infests bay trees, citrus plants, *Schefflera*, *Ficus*, and many other plants. The flat, oval, yellowish brown scales are up to 3mm (1/8in) long, and clustered along the larger veins on the underside of leaves. Infested plants are sticky with honeydew and often develop sooty moulds. Spray with thiacloprid, acetamiprid, fatty acids, or plant oils.

Tarsonemid mite

The microscopic mites suck sap from tissues developing inside the growing points and flower buds of many glasshouse plants. This damage stunts the growth, causing scarring on the stems and leaves, and deformed spoon-shaped leaves. Flower buds often abort. There is no treatment, so once the diagnosis has been confirmed, dispose of infested plants.

Glasshouse thrips

Several species of thrips suck sap from glasshouse plants. Adult thrips are yellowish brown or black and have narrow elongate bodies, 2mm (1/12in) long. The nymphs are creamy white and cause a pale mottling on the leaves and flowers. Because of their size, thrips often hide in inaccessible places on plants. Use a systemic insecticide, such as thiacloprid or acetamiprid.

Glasshouse pests and diseases *continued*

Glasshouse leafhopper
The adults are 3mm (⅛in) long with mottled yellow and grey markings. The adults and the creamy white nymphs suck sap from the underside of leaves of tomato, cucumber, and many ornamental plants, causing a coarse pale mottling of the upper leaf surface. Control by spraying with thiacloprid, acetamiprid, bifenthrin, pyrethrum, plant oils, or fatty acids.

Mealybug
Cacti, succulents, and many other glasshouse plants are attacked by these sap-sucking insects. They infest relatively inaccessible places on their host plants and are covered with a white waxy secretion. Heavily infested plants are weakened with honeydew. Spray with thiacloprid, acetamiprid, fatty acids, or plant oils, or use a ladybird, *Cryptolaemus*, as a biocontrol.

Root mealybug
These white, sap-sucking insects feed on the roots of pot plants. They are up to 2mm (½₂in) long, which is about half the size of mealybugs that feed on the foliage. A white waxy powder coats the roots and soil particles where they are present. Treat infested plants with acetamiprid or thiacloprid products sold as a compost drench for vine weevil control.

Springtails
These harmless wingless insects often occur in potting compost. They are up to 3mm (⅛in) long and often white. They are most frequently seen when a pot plant is watered as this flushes springtails up onto the surface or out of the pot's drainage hole. They feed on decaying plant material and the associated fungal growth, so they do not damage plants.

Vine weevil grubs
Vine weevil grubs are creamy white, legless, and up to 10mm (½in) long. They eat plant roots and bore into begonia and cyclamen tubers. Most pot plants are vulnerable and can be killed during autumn to spring. Use a compost drench of thiacloprid or acetamiprid in late summer, or apply a pathogenic nematode, *Steinernema kraussei*, as a biocontrol.

Carnation tortrix moth
Two species, carnation tortrix and light brown apple moth, have pale green caterpillars, up to 18mm (¾in) long, that attack many glasshouse and garden plants. The caterpillars bind two leaves together or fold a leaf with silk threads and graze the inner leaf surfaces. Concealed larvae are difficult to reach, so squeeze bound up leaves to crush the caterpillars.

Fungus gnats

These greyish black flies, 3–4mm (⅛in) long, run over or fly around seed trays or pot plants. The larvae are white, slender maggots with black heads, up to 5mm (¼in) long. They feed mainly on dead roots but can damage seedlings and soft cuttings. Control adults with sticky yellow traps. Predatory mites and a nematode are available as biocontrols.

Aphids

Most glasshouse plants attract aphids, which may be green, pink, black, or mottled. They suck sap, weakening and distorting growth. Plants are soiled with honeydew, sooty moulds, and white cast skins. Spray with thiacloprid, bifenthrin, acetamiprid, pyrethrum, plant oils, or fatty acids. Predators and parasitic wasps are available as biocontrols.

Orchid viruses

Viruses are a common problem on orchids, but most of them are rare. The most important orchid viruses are cymbidium mosaic virus and odontoglossum ringspot virus. Foliar symptoms range from chlorotic streaks to black necrotic spots and line patterns. As there are no cures for viruses, destroy plants and disinfect work areas and tools.

Damping off

Seedlings collapse at soil level and roots may be decayed. Damping off is caused by soil- and water-borne organisms such as *Pythium*. To reduce the incidence, use sterile compost and cleaned seedling trays. Sow seeds thinly and use tap water. If damping off occurs, remove affected seedlings and water the remainder with copper oxychloride.

Glasshouse viruses

Plants exhibit a range of symptoms when infected by viruses (*see p.41*). Under glass, three viruses are very common, and all have a wide host range. Cucumber mosaic virus (CMV) (*see p.119*) is often on begonias. Impatiens necrotic spot virus (INSV) is vectored by western flower thrips. It can affect a huge range of plants causing diverse symptoms. Tomato spotted wilt virus (TSWV) is also vectored by western flower thrips. In dahlias it typically produces an "oakleaf"-type ringspot pattern. Viruses cannot be cured and affected plants must be destroyed. In glasshouses where viruses are present, it is important to sterilize cutting tools when propagating. The pest population must also be controlled.

Index

A

Abies 68
Acacia 137
acanthus powdery mildew
  45, 96
Acer 43, 67, 70, 72, 80, 85
  pimple gall 46, 70
  tar spot 44, 70
acid soil 10, 14, 15
acorn gall wasp 73
adelgids 67
air circulation 20, 40, 91,
  100, 135
alkaline soil 10, 14, 15, 23
alliums 46, 120
anemone 91
  smut 45, 101
annuals 9, 98–9
anthocorid bugs 61
anthracnose 44, 71, 74, 94,
  113
antirrhinum rust 46, 97
ants 28, 30, 104
aphids 9, 27, 28, 31, 47, 76,
  85, 86, 93, 94, 96, 113,
  122, 123, 124, 125, 139
  bark aphid 75
  blister aphid 47, 126
  controls 52, 54, 61, 62, 63
  mealy aphid 115, 125
  root aphid 27, 33, 47, 118
  virus vectors 30, 32, 119
apple 15, 69, 110, 111,
  122–123
  canker 49, 68, 123
  capsid bugs 31, 122
  codling moth 122
  leaf-mining moth 46, 122
  rosy apple aphid 122
  sawfly 122
apricot 124
arbutus leaf spots 44, 70
ash 68
asparagus beetle 30, 47, 121
aubergine 109
auriculas 33, 92
azalea 10, 46, 82

B

bacterial shothole 77
badgers 35, 104

bark 16, 20, 36, 37
barriers 58, 135
bay 137
  powdery mildew 45, 130
  sucker 46, 130
bean 9, 15, 23, 33, 36, 91,
  109, 112–113
  anthracnose 44, 113
  black aphid 47, 113
  chocolate spot 44, 113
  halo blight 44, 113
  rust 46, 113
  seed fly 113
  weevil 47, 112
  yellow mosaic virus 97
beech 43, 68
  woolly aphid 47, 70
bees 9, 60, 93, 104, 109
  leaf-cutting 31, 47, 86
beet leaf miner 46, 121
beetles 27, 28, 30, 32, 34, 47,
  81, 93, 100, 108, 114, 121,
  128, 129, 130, 131
beetroot 120, 121
begonias 136, 138, 139
beneficial creatures 52
berberis sawfly 47, 78
Betula, see beech
biological controls 63, 134,
  135
birds 9, 27, 35, 37, 48, 59, 62,
  104, 110, 111, 115
black bean aphid 47, 113
blackberry 127, 128
blackbirds 111
blackcurrant: big bud mite
  126
  gall midge 126
blackfly 29, 31, 124
black spot 13, 87
blight 116, 117, 119, 127, 128
blossom end rot 15
blossom wilt 48, 111
box 43, 80
bracket fungi 39, 42, 43, 69
branches, removing 20, 21
brassica collars 59, 115
brassicas 14, 23, 28, 37, 59,
  109, 114–115
  flea beetles 47, 114
  downy mildew 45, 114
  leaf spot 44, 114
  ring spot 44, 114

broccoli 23
broom gall mite 48, 78
brown rot 48, 123
brown scale 46, 49, 110
buddleia 78, 79, 92
buds 48, 111
big bud 66
bud blast 83
bulb scale mite 100
bulbs 9, 10, 13, 37, 100–103
  rot 102, 103
bullfinches 111
bumblebees 60, 109
busy lizzie 98
buttercup, creeping 101
butterflies 9, 28, 30, 47, 115

C

cabbage 23, 28, 37, 114–115
  mealy aphid 48, 115
  moth 115
  root fly 27, 49, 59, 115
  whitefly 47, 115
cabbage white butterfly 28,
  47, 98, 115
cacti 138
cages 110, 115
calcium 14, 15
camellia 10, 14, 66, 82
  galls 46, 82
  petal blight 82
  viruses 45, 48, 82
canker 48, 49, 68, 75, 87,
  111, 117, 123
  bacterial 47, 49, 124
  bleeding 39, 42, 49, 72
canna 41, 45, 97
capsid bugs 27, 31, 48, 122
carnation tortrix moth 138
carrot 23, 33, 35, 59, 117
  fly 27, 49, 59, 121
caterpillars 9, 26, 27, 28, 29,
  30
  control methods 52, 66
  moth 32, 67, 79, 90, 92,
  110, 115, 118, 120, 138
cats 27, 35
cauliflower 23
celeriac 120, 121
celery 117, 120
  leaf miner 46, 121
  leaf spot 44, 121

centipedes 62
Chaenomeles 78, 123
chafer grubs 27, 33, 35, 49,
  63, 104
chemicals 52–55
cherry 110, 124
  blackfly 47, 124
  leaf scorch 44, 47, 124
  leaf spot 44, 47, 124
  slugworm 47, 123
choosing plants 12–13, 14
chrysanthemum 31, 91
  leaf miner 46, 95
  rust 46, 95
cineraria 92, 95, 98
citrus plants 137
clay soil 14
clematis 31, 84
  slime flux 49, 84
  wilt 47, 84
climate 10
climbers 84–5
cloches 36, 59
clubroot 23, 47, 49, 109
coastal gardens 10
codling moth 27, 57, 122
Colorado beetle 47, 108
companion planting 9, 22
compost 16, 17
conifers 45, 67, 76–77
containers 19, 23, 33, 58
controls 51–63
  biological 63, 134
  integrated 135
copper tape 58
coral spot 20, 49, 67
Cordyline 36
corms 13, 36, 37, 100–103
coryneum canker 49, 68
Cotoneaster 69, 111
  webber moth 47, 79
crocus 36, 37, 101
crop rotation 9, 23, 33, 109
crown gall 49, 68
cuckoo spit 31, 131
cucumber 136, 138
  mosaic virus 45, 119, 139
  powdery mildew 45, 119
cultivation 7–23, 52, 135
currant 67, 126
  blister aphid 47, 126
  leaf spot 44, 126
cushion scale 32, 46, 66–67

cutworms 27, 49, 108
cyclamen 136, 138
cypress aphid 47, 76

D

daffodils 36, 102
dahlia 31, 41, 139
    smut 44, 103
damping off 47, 49, 139
damsons 125
deer 27, 36, 59
delphinium 36
    black blotch 44, 95
    powdery mildew 45, 95
dianthus smut 48, 95
die-back 39, 41, 43, 85, 87
diseases 38–43
disinfectant 19
dogs 27, 35
dogwood anthracnose 44, 71
downy mildew 23, 40, 45, 81,
    86, 98, 99, 112, 114, 118
drought-tolerant plants 10
Dutch elm disease 47, 49, 71

E

earwigs 27, 28, 29, 31, 84
eelworms 23, 27, 33, 34, 92,
    102, 116
    leaf and bud 44, 45, 91
Eleagnus 67
elephant hawk moth 47, 79
elm: bark beetle 71
    Dutch elm disease 47, 49,
    71
    gall mite 46, 71
equipment 54
escallonia leaf spots 44, 77
eucalyptus 46, 47, 71
euonymus scale 46, 49, 80

F

fairy rings 105
fallen material 18, 19, 40, 70
feeding 19, 40
felt galls 66
fencing 35, 36
fertilizers 14, 16, 19, 23, 43, 87
fig 67, 137
figwort weevil 47, 79

fireblight 47, 48, 111
flea beetles 47, 114
flies 28, 34, 63, 113, 120, 121
flower bugs 61
flowers 9, 19, 48
fluted scale 46, 137
foliar diseases 38, 40–41
foliar feeds 83
foliar scabs 41
foxes 27, 35, 104
freesias 92, 97
fritillaries 100
frogs 9, 62
fruit 15, 19, 27, 36, 37, 41,
    60, 110–111
    symptoms 48–49
fruit cages 110
fruit trees 9, 56, 68, 110–111,
    122–125
fuchsia 46, 79
fungi 13, 18, 19, 38, 39,
    42–43
fungicides 13, 40, 52, 91
fungus gnats 56, 139
Fusarium 23, 39, 43, 47, 49,
    116

G

gall midges 48, 78, 93, 94,
    123, 126
gall mites 34, 46, 48, 66, 74,
    78, 125, 126, 127
gall wasps 71, 73
galls 27, 30, 46, 48, 49, 66,
    82, 86
garlic 120
geranium:
    powdery mildew 45, 94
    sawfly 47, 94
gerbera 92, 95, 98
geum sawfly 47, 93
gladiolus 45, 92, 97, 100
glasshouse 29, 34, 56, 85,
    133–139
gleditsia gall midge 46, 78
globeflower 101
gloves 55
gooseberry 67, 126
    American mildew 45, 48, 27
    leaf spot 44
    sawfly 47, 127
graft failure 85

grape 110, 126, 136
    erinose mite 45, 127
grass 9; see also lawns
grease bands 56, 110
green spruce aphid 76
greenfly 29, 31, 63, 86
greenhouse, see glasshouse
grey mould 41, 48, 49, 129,
    131, 135, 136

H

hawthorn 69, 70, 111, 123
    webber moth 79
heather 10, 16
hebe downy mildew 45, 81
hedges 10, 76–77
hellebore: black death 45, 96
    leaf blotch 44, 96
hemerocallis 100
    gall midge 48, 94
hemispherical scale 46, 49,
    137
herbaceous plants 9, 29, 36,
    90–91
herbs 130–131
herons 37
Hippeastrum 100, 102
holly 66, 68
    leaf blight 44, 77
    leaf miner 44, 46, 76
hollyhock rust 44, 46, 97
holm oak leaf miner 46, 73
honeydew 30, 31, 32
honey fungus 39, 42, 43, 47,
    49, 74, 85, 86
honeysuckle: aphid 48, 85
    powdery mildew 45, 85
horse chestnut:
    bleeding canker 49, 72
    leaf blotch 44, 72
    leaf-mining moth 46, 72
    scale 46, 49, 72
horticultural fleece 59, 115,
    120, 121
houseplants 29, 134
hoverflies 9, 52, 61, 63
hydrangea 18–19, 36, 65
    scale 46, 49, 80

I J

Impatiens: downy mildew
    45, 98

necrotic spot virus 130
insecticides 52
insects 9, 22, 27, 33, 34, 39
iris 103
ink disease 101
    leaf spot 44, 101
    rust 46, 101
    sawfly 47, 101
iron 14, 15
ivy leaf spot 44, 84
juniper 76

K

kale 23
Keithia thujina needle blight
    77

L

laburnum leaf miner 46, 78
lacebugs 80
lacewings 52, 61, 63
ladybirds 30, 52, 62, 63,
    134
larch 67
laurel 43, 77
Lavatera 44, 92, 97
lavender 31, 130, 131
    grey mould 49, 131
lawns 35, 36, 89, 104–105
leaf blight 39, 42, 44, 74,
    83
leaf-cutting bees 31, 47
leafhoppers 27, 30, 32, 45,
    83, 87, 129, 138
leaf miners 27, 30, 32, 78,
    79, 92, 95, 120, 121, 122
leaf spot 38, 39, 40, 44, 47,
    70, 77, 81, 83, 84, 99,
    114,121, 124, 126, 129
leatherjackets 27, 49, 63,
    104
leaves 18, 19, 29
    foliar diseases 38, 40–41
    symptoms 15, 44–48
leek: moth 46, 120
    white tip 44, 120
lettuce 33, 108
    downy mildew 40, 45,
    118
    root aphid 47, 118
    viruses 45, 118

Index

lilac 76, 78
lily 103
  beetle 30, 47, 100
  disease 44, 48, 100
lime 70, 72
  nail gall mite 46, 72
loganberry 128
lovage 121
lupin: anthracnose 44, 94
  aphid 48, 94

M

maggots 28, 113, 115, 120, 123
magnesium deficiency 15
Magnolia 67
Mahonia 78
  rust 46, 81
mammals 27, 35–37, 47, 56, 62
manganese deficiency 15
manures 16, 23
maples 70
marguerite daisy 92, 95, 98
marigolds 9
marjoram 130, 131
mealybug ladybirds 134
mealybugs 27, 28, 30, 46, 62, 92, 138
  root 47, 138
metamorphosis 28
mice 27, 36, 56, 101
Michaelmas daisy mite 48, 93
midges 52, 63
mildew 9, 13, 127
  see also downy mildew; powdery mildew
millipedes 27, 33, 34, 128
mint: beetle 47, 131
  rust 46, 131
mites 27, 28, 30, 34, 93, 100, 127, 128, 137
  predatory 134, 139
moles 36, 56, 57, 104
moths 28, 30, 32, 34, 47, 67, 90, 92, 110, 112, 115, 118, 120, 125, 138
mountain ash gall mite 74
mulberry 126
  blight 44, 127
  leaf spot 44, 127

mulches 10, 14, 16, 40, 82, 94
mullein 79, 92
mushrooms 43
mustard 23

N

nail galls 46, 66, 72
narcissus 100
  basal rot 102
  bulb fly 102
  eelworm 102
  leaf scorch 103
  smoulder 102
  white mould 103
necrosis 15, 41
nectar robbing 109
nectarine 110, 124
nematodes 27, 32, 33, 34, 39, 91, 92, 102, 116
  pathogenic 63, 90, 104, 134, 138, 139
netting 35, 37, 59, 110, 115
  wire 36, 58
nettles 52, 101
newts 9
Nicotiana 45, 99
night 26, 29, 31, 32
nitrogen 14, 15, 17, 23, 113
nurseries, specialist 13
nutrients 14–15, 16, 19
nuts 37

O

oak: gall wasps 46, 73
  powdery mildew 45, 73
  processionary moth 47, 73
oleander scale 46, 137
olive 69
onion 33, 108, 120
  fly 49, 120
  neck rot 121
  white rot 120
orchid viruses 45, 139
organic matter 14, 16, 17, 23
overwintering 29

P

pansy: downy mildew 45, 99
  leaf spots 44, 99
  sickness 47, 49, 99

parsley 23, 120, 121
parsnip 23, 35, 117, 120, 121
  canker 23, 117
  viruses 45, 117
passion flower virus 45, 85
pea 23, 36, 37, 91, 97, 112–113
  mildew 45, 112
  moth 112
  thrips 23, 45, 112
  weevil 47, 112
peach 110, 124
  leaf curl 46, 124
pear 69, 111, 122–123
  bedstraw aphid 48, 123
  brown rot 123
  canker 49, 68, 123
  fruitlet midge 123
  rust 46, 123
  slugworm 47, 123
pelargonium rust 46, 94, 135
penstemon 91
peony wilt 44, 49, 96
perennials 92–97
periwinkle rust 46, 97
Pestalotiopsis 77
pesticides 29, 33, 52, 53, 55, 135
pests 26–37
  above ground 27, 30–32
  lifecycles 28–29
  mammals and birds 35–37
  soil-dwelling 27, 33
petunia viruses 45, 48, 99
pH test 14, 23
pheromone traps 57, 122, 125
phlox eelworm 92
Phomopsis die-back 74
phormium mealybug 46, 92
phosphorus 14, 15
Phygelius 78, 79
Phytophthora 39, 42, 47, 49, 74, 77, 83, 85, 120, 131
pieris lacebug 45, 80
pigeons 27, 37, 115
pine 67
plane anthracnose 44, 74
planting 19
plum 110, 111, 123, 124
  gall mite 46, 125
  leaf-curling aphid 48, 125
  mealy aphid 48, 125

moth 125
  pocket plum 125
  sawfly 125
pollinators 9, 31, 60, 109
ponds 9, 37, 62, 93, 101
poplar 49, 75
pot plants 138
potassium 14, 15
potato 23, 33, 68, 108, 109, 117–118
  blackleg 116
  blight 44, 117
  common scab 116
  cyst eelworm 23, 116
  dry rot 116
  early blight 116
  gangrene 117
  silver scurf 117
  spraing 23, 117
powdery mildew 39, 40, 45, 48, 73, 77, 83, 85, 86, 91, 94, 95, 96, 98, 112, 119, 128, 130, 136
  control methods 53
powdery scab 23
privet 76, 78
pruning 20–21, 65, 87
Prunus 43, 47, 68, 80, 85, 111, 124–125
Pyracantha 69, 111
  leaf miner 46, 79
Pythium 39, 99, 139

Q R

quince leaf blight 44, 48, 74
rabbits 27, 36, 56, 57, 58, 59
radish 23, 114, 115, 118, 120
raspberry 91, 128–129
  beetle 30, 128
  leaf and bud mite 45, 128
  powdery mildew 45, 128
  rust 46, 129
rats 27, 36, 56
red berry mite 127
red spider mite 45, 61, 62, 76, 111, 134, 136
redcurrant 126, 127
repellent substances 35
resistant plants 13, 42, 43, 135
rhizomes 100–103

rhododendron 10, 14, 66, 80, 82, 83
  bud blast 83
  leaf blight 44, 83
  leafhopper 83
  leaf spots 44, 83
  powdery mildew 45, 83
  rust 46, 83
ring spot 23
Robin's pin cushion 86
Robinia decline 44, 49, 74
rocket 114
root aphids 27, 33, 47, 118
root fly maggots 33, 115
root mealybugs 47, 138
root problems 14, 33, 42
root rot 39, 42, 47, 49
root vegetables 23, 33, 36, 108
rose 13, 31, 49, 86–87
  aphid 48, 86
  black spot 44, 87
  canker and die-back 49, 87
  leafhopper 45, 87
  rust 13, 46, 87
  sawflies 47, 86
  viruses 45, 87
rosemary beetle 47, 130
rot 39, 42–43, 69, 102, 103, 116, 120, 121, 123
rowan (*Sorbus*) 68, 69, 70, 74, 78, 111, 123
rust 13, 38, 39, 40, 41, 46, 79, 81, 83, 87, 94, 95, 97, 101, 113, 129, 131, 135
  chemical controls 52

S

safety 55
sage leafhopper 45, 130
salad crops 118–119
Salix, see willow
sandy soil 10, 14, 15
savory 130, 131
sawflies 27, 28, 30, 32, 34, 47, 75, 78, 86, 92, 93, 94, 101, 122, 125, 127
scabs 45, 48, 69, 116
scale insects 27, 28, 30, 32, 46, 49, 62, 66, 80, 85, 137
scaring devices 35, 36, 37, 59, 115
Schefflera 137

Sclerotinia 42, 47, 49
seedlings 19, 29, 33, 34, 36, 58, 59, 108, 109, 139
seeds 39
sempervivum leaf miner 46, 92
shade 10, 135
shrews 62
shrubs 66–7, 78–81
silver fir 76, 79
silver leaf disease 20, 43, 46
slime flux 49, 84
slime moulds 105
slugs 9, 27, 28, 29, 33, 34, 47, 49, 135
  controls 53, 56, 58, 59, 62, 63, 134
slugworms 86, 123
smut 41, 45, 48, 95, 101, 103
snails 27, 28, 29, 34, 47
  controls 53, 56, 58, 59, 62
snowdrop 102
  grey mould 49, 103
snow mould 105
soft fruit 32, 126–129
soft scale 46, 49, 137
soil 10, 14–17
  pests 27, 33
  pH 14, 23
Solomon's seal sawfly 47, 92
song thrush 62
sooty mould 30, 31, 32
Sorbus, see rowan
southern green shield bug 91
spores 39
sprays and sprayers 53, 54
springtails 138
spruce 67, 76
squirrels 27, 37, 56, 101
stems 27, 39, 48–49
sterilizing 19, 85, 99
strawberry 128–129
  green petal 129
  grey mould 48, 49, 129
  leaf spot 44, 129
seed beetle 129
  viruses 45, 129
succulents 138
sucker 28, 30, 47, 61, 80, 130
sulphur 14, 53
swede 23, 114, 115, 116, 120
sweetcorn 35, 36, 37
sweet pea mildew 45, 98
swift moth caterpillars 90

Swiss chard 120, 121
sycamore 70, 72
symptoms 27, 40, 44–49

T

tarsonemid mite 137
thrips 27, 28, 30, 32, 34, 45, 56, 100, 112, 137, 139
Thuja 77
thyme 130
tits 9, 52
toads 9, 62
toadstools 39, 69, 105
tobacco, *see Nicotiana*
tomato 23, 91, 109, 136, 138
  blight 44, 119
  blossom end rot 15
  ghost spot 48, 118
  leaf mould 119
  moth 47, 118
  potassium deficiency 15
  viruses 45, 119, 139
tools 19, 21
tortrix moth 47, 90, 138
Trachelospermum 66
traps 56–57, 84, 104, 122, 125, 135
tree guards 36, 58
tree scabs 45, 48, 69
trees 10, 65, 66–67, 70–75
  bark stripping 36, 37
  pruning 20
  symptoms 48–49
tubers 100–103
tulip 37, 101
  fire 49, 103
turf: fairy rings 105
  red thread 105
turnip 23, 33, 114, 115, 116, 120

V

vegetables 9, 14, 22–23, 36, 37, 58, 108–9, 112–121
verbascum 92
Verticillium wilt 39, 43, 47, 49, 85
viburnum: beetle 20, 47, 81
  whitefly 48, 81
vine weevil 34, 47
  grubs 27, 33, 49, 63, 138

violet gall midge 46, 93
viruses 38, 40, 41, 45, 48, 82, 85, 87, 97, 99, 117, 118, 119, 129, 139
  vectors 30, 32, 39

W

walnut gall mite 46, 74
washing-up liquid 54
wasps 32, 57
  parasitic 63, 134, 136
watering 15, 19, 40, 135
watering cans 54, 55
water lily: aphid 48, 93
  beetle 47, 93
weeds 16, 19, 105, 117, 129
weevils 79, 112
white blister 23, 46, 109
whitefly 27, 28, 30, 34, 47, 81, 115, 134, 136
  traps 56
white mould 42, 103
wildlife 9, 35–37
willow (*Salix*) 68, 69
  anthracnose 44, 75
  bark aphid 75
  bean gall sawfly 46, 75
  black canker 44, 75
  leaf beetle 47, 75
willow herb 79
wilt 39, 42–43, 47, 49, 84, 96
winter 29, 37
winter moth 47, 56, 110
wireworms 27, 33, 49, 108
wisteria: die-back 47, 49, 85
  scale 46, 49, 85
witches' broom 48, 68
wood chippings 15
wood decay fungi 20, 39, 49, 69
woodlice 27, 28, 33, 34, 62
woolly aphids 47, 79
worms 16, 17, 62, 105
wounds 20, 21, 39, 67, 68

Y

yew 43
  root rot 49, 77
Yucca 36
  leaf spot 44, 81

Acknowledgements

The publisher would like to thank the Royal Horticultural Society for their kind permission to reproduce the following photographs in this book:

(Key: a-above; b-below/bottom; c-centre; l-left; r-right; t-top)

1, **5** (tr) (br). **27** (br). **29** (br). **30** (c). **31** (bl) (cr). **32** (bl). **33** (tr) (br). **38**. **39** (tr) (bl) (br). **40** (bl) (br). **41** (tr) (bl) (cl) (cr) (br). **42** (bl) (r). **43** (tr) (bl) (c) (br). **44** (l); (r).**45** (l) (c); (r). **46** (l) (c) (r). **47** (l) (c) (r). **48** (c) (r). **49** (l) (c) (r). **56** (tr) (bl). **57** (br). **59** (tr). **60** (bl) (tr). **61** (bl). **63** (br). **64-65**. **66** (tr) (bl); (br). **67** (bl). **68** (tr) (bl) (br). **69** (tr) (bl). **70** (cl) (tr) (bl) (br). **71** (tl) (tc) (bl) (bc) (r). **72** (l) (tr) (bc) (br). **73** (tl) (bl) (bc) (br). **74** (tc) (bl) (bc) (br). **75** (tc) (br). **76** (tc) (tr) (bl) (bc) (br). **77** (tl) (tc) (tr) (bl) (bc); (br). **78** (tc) (bl) (bc) (br). **79** (tl) (tc) (tr) (bl). **80** (tl) (tc) (tr) (bl) (br). **81** (tc) (bl) (bc) (r). **82** (l) (tr) (bc) (br). **83** (tc) (tr) (bc) (br). **84** (tr) (bl). **85** (l) (tc) (bc) (br). **86** (tc) (bl) (bc) (br). **87** (tl) (bl) (bc) (br). **90** (tr) (b). **91** (tr) (br). **92** (tc) (tr) (bl) (bc) (br). **93** (tl) (bl) (bc) (br). **94** (tl) (tc) (tr) (bl) (bc) (br). **95** (tl) (tc) (tr) (bl). **96** (tl) (tr) (bl). **97** (tr) (bl) (br). **98** (t) (bl). **99** (tl) (tc) (bl). **100** (tc) (tr) (br). **101** (tc) (bl) (bc) (br). **102** (l) (tc) (tr); **103** (tl) (tr) (bl) (bc) (br). **104** (tr) (bl) (bc) (br). **105** (tl) (tc) (tr) (bl) (br). **108** (tl) (bl) (br). **109** (tl) (bl) (br). **110** (tl) (bl) (br). **111** (tr) (bl) (br). **112** (tc) (bl) (br). **113** (tc) (tr) (bl) (bc). **114** (tc) (br). **115** (tl) (tc) (tr) (bl) (bc) (br). **116** (tc) (tr) (bc) (br). **117** (tc) (bc). **118** (tc) (tr) (bc) (br). **119** (tl) (bc). **120** (tc) (bc). **121** (tl) (bl) (bc). **122** (tc) (tr) (bl) (bc) (br). **123** (tl) (tr) (bl) (bc) (br). **124** (tc) (tr) (bl) (bc) (br). **125** (tl) (tc) (tr) (bc) (br). **126** (tc) (r) (bl) (bc). **127** (tl) (tc) (tr) (bc) (br). **128** (tc) (tr) (bl) (bc) (br). **129** (tl) (tc) (tr). **131** (bl); (bc) (r). **136** (tr) (br). **137** (tl) (tc) (tr) (bl) (bc)(br). **138** (tl) (tc) (tr) (bl) (bc) (br). **139** (tl) (tr) (br).

The publisher also wishes to thank the following for their kind permission to reproduce their photographs:

6 Photolibrary: Rod Edwards. **8** Photolibrary: Dave Porter. **9** Alamy Images: David Robertson (t). FLPA: Gary K. Smith (c). Photolibrary: Eric Crichton (bl); Juliette Wade (br). **10** Photolibrary: Juliette Wade. **11** Alamy Images: John Glover (tr). Photolibrary: Carole Drake (cr); Andrea Jones (br). **12** Science Photo Library: Brian Gadsby. **15** FLPA: Nigel Cattlin (tl) (tc). **18** Alamy Images: Andrea Jones. **27** NHPA / Photoshot: Photo Researchers (bl). **28** FLPA: Minden Pictures/Silvia Reiche (br). Getty Images: Taxi/Jan Tove Johansson (bc). naturepl.com: Gary K. Smith (bl). NHPA / Photoshot: Laurie Campbell (t). **29** Corbis: Jacqui Hurst (bl). Dorling Kindersley: Kim Taylor (t). **31** Alamy Images: Andrew Darrington (br). Dorling Kindersley: Emma Callery (clb). **32** Alamy Images: Bruce Coleman Inc (tl); Nigel Cattlin (br). FLPA: Richard Becker (bc); Malcolm Schuyl (tc). **33** Photolibrary: Donald Specker (bl). **34** Ardea: John Cancalosi (t). FLPA: Nigel Cattlin (bl) (br). **35** Corbis: Jeff Vanuga (tr). FLPA: Martin B. Withers (br). **36** Corbis: FLPA/Peter Reynolds (tl); image100 (tr); Robert Harding World Imagery/Steve & Ann Toon (br). **37** Alamy Images: botanikfoto/Steffen Hauser (br). Dorling Kindersley: Dan Bannister (t). Getty Images: DeAgostini/L. Andena (bl). **41** FLPA: Nigel Cattlin (br). **44** Dorling Kindersley: Emma Callery (bc). **52** GAP Photos: Dave Bevan (l). **53** Alamy Images: Wild Places Photography/Chris Howes (bl). Photolibrary: Michael Howes (br). **58** Dorling Kindersley: Emma Callery (br). **61** Ardea: Geoff du Feu (br). FLPA: Minden/FotoNatura (t). **62** FLPA: Minden Pictures/Silvia Reiche; Roger Wilmshurst (br); Martin B. Withers (tc). Photolibrary: Barrie Watts (tr). **63** FLPA: Nigel Cattlin (t) (bl). **72** FLPA: Nigel Cattlin (tc). **73** FLPA: ImageBroker (tr). **75** Garden World Images: T. Schilling (tl). **79** FLPA: Nigel Cattlin (br). **81** Dorling Kindersley: Emma Callery (tl). **83** Kenneth Cox: (bl). FLPA: Nigel Cattlin (tl). **86** Dorling Kindersley: Emma Callery (tr). **87** Dorling Kindersley: Emma Callery (tr). **91** FLPA: Nigel Cattlin (bl). **93** FLPA: Nigel Cattlin (tr). **95** FLPA: Nigel Cattlin (br). **96** Dorling Kindersley: Emma Callery (br). **97** Dorling Kindersley: Emma Callery (tl). **98** GardenPhotos.com: Judy White (br). **99** FLPA: Nigel Cattlin (bc) (br). **101** FLPA: Nigel Cattlin (bl). photo Petr Kokeš, Czechia: (tr). **102** FLPA: Nigel Cattlin (tr). Photoshot: Photos Horticultural/Michael Warren (br). **103** FLPA: Nigel Cattlin (tr). **104** Corbis: image100 (tl). **105** FLPA: Roger Wilmshurst (bc). **112** FLPA: Nigel Cattlin (br). Garden World Images: Dave Bevan (bc). **113** FLPA: Nigel Cattlin (tl). Garden World Images: MAP/Mise au Point (br). **114** FLPA: Nigel Cattlin (tr) (bl). **117** Alamy Images: Nigel Cattlin (bl). FLPA: Nigel Cattlin (tr). GAP Photos: Dave Bevan (tl). Garden World Images: Dave Bevan (br). **118** FLPA: Nigel Cattlin (bl). **119** FLPA: Nigel Cattlin (tr) (br). **120** FLPA: Nigel Cattlin (bl). **121** FLPA: Nigel Cattlin (br). **129** FLPA: Nigel Cattlin (bl) (bc). Science Photo Library: Dr Jeremy Burgess (br). **130** Dorling Kindersley: Emma Callery (bl). FLPA: Nigel Cattlin (tr) (br). **134** Alamy Images: Nigel Cattlin (br). FLPA: Nigel Cattlin (tl) (bl) (tr). **135** Alamy Images: Mark Boulton (br); David Chapman (tl); Carole Hewer (bc). **136** Corbis: Tim Graham (l). **139** FLPA: Nigel Cattlin (tr) (bc)

Jacket images: Front and Back: FLPA: Nigel Cattlin GAP Photos: Maxine Adcock Zara Napier

All other images © Dorling Kindersley For further information see: **www.dkimages.com**

Dorling Kindersley would also like to thank the following:

RHS Editor: Simon Maughan
RHS Picture Research: Ian Waghorn
Index: Chris Bernstein